I WOULDN'T CHANGE A THING

I WOULDN'T CHANGE A THING

How my daughter embraced life with cancer as an unexpected adventure

To Wendy —
Wishing you love, laughter and ladybugs!
Gina

GINA M. PECA

All proceeds from this book benefit the Catie Hoch
Foundation.

www.catiehochfoundation.org
"Helping kids take a break from cancer."

This book is dedicated to my beautiful daughter Catie
and my wonderful husband Larry.
I miss you both every day and love you more
than you could ever know.

A special thank you to Robyn Ringler of Eastline
Books in Clifton Park, New York for giving me the
confidence to put words to paper. To Robyn Silverman,
thank you for taking so much time to read and edit
the book. I am so grateful for all of your efforts. To
my sister, Terry Peca-Baker, thank you for your careful
reading and helpful comments. Your assistance was
invaluable.

Contents

Prologue

I met my husband Larry on a blind date. A friend from law school was working with Larry. She gave him my number and he called me. We decided to meet at St. Andrew's Plaza in lower Manhattan. He told me he would be the tall guy in a suit. (How many thousands of tall guys in suits are there in New York City?) But we found each other. Fourteen months later we were married. I was pregnant by our first anniversary.

Larry was working at the IRS. I was a prosecutor for the New York State Education Department. Although we really loved New York City, we both knew that we did not want to raise our children there.

Larry started interviewing and immediately got a job offer with GE in the Albany area. I was thrilled because my sister and her husband lived in the area. Six weeks after Catie was born in 1991, Larry and I moved upstate. We bought a house and a puppy and Larry started his new job as a corporate tax attorney. People say that these things are some of the most stressful events in a person's life, but all we felt was happy and lucky. Our daughter was beautiful and we loved our new life.

I always said that if I had children, I would take six weeks off and then go right back to work. *Not going to happen.* I had Catie in 1991 and then Robby in 1992. Johnny was born in 1995. I did some sporadic work as a Law Guardian in Saratoga County Family Court, but my heart was home with my kids. We were doing fine on Larry's salary, so after Johnny came along I stopped working. So I was a stay-at-home mom.

Catie was pure sunshine. With a bright and bubbly personality, she was a charmer. When she was just a baby, we brought her to Babyland to pick out a crib. She was about four months old. She chattered the whole time we were in the store. She wasn't speaking any real words, but she didn't seem to notice. The salespeople were laughing, telling us to watch out, that our phone bills were going to be huge when she was a teenager.

She was a daredevil. In nursery school, all she wanted to do was swing like a chimpanzee from rung to rung on the playground monkey bars. When it came time to ride the pony at the end of the year picnic, it was all Larry could do to keep up with her.

She was a good big sister, she loved her little brothers, but she had her moments. Playing game after game of Candyland with her, we had to teach her how to be a good sport. It looked like it was killing her to shake hands and say "good game" after she lost.

She was always excited about something. That sense of excitement stayed with her throughout her life. This is a story about Catie. It's about Catie's love of life, cancer and all. As we began the journey to save her life, she was all about living her life. While I became consumed with the trauma she was going through, she was consumed with simply living her life, the way she always did by finding delight in everything she did, disregarding the roadblocks, and staying open to the possibilities of each new day. At some point during this journey, I realized that my daughter had become my teacher. This is the story of how Catie changed my world.

Chapter 1

Life Is Good

As my life as a parent began, I often didn't recognize just how lucky I was. I knew that I was blessed with three healthy children and a wonderful husband. But those are things easily taken for granted. It was only when something changed that I realized how fortunate I had been.

On a gorgeous sunny Saturday in August 1997, we were celebrating our youngest child's birthday. Johnny was turning two. We had family and friends over to the house for a cookout. A slip and slide was set up in the front yard. On the grill in the backyard was a whole filet mignon. Kids were running around. We were all just relaxing. Catie was six years old. Robby was four. It was suburban heaven.

During the party, Catie came into the kitchen. "Mom, I fell on the slip and slide and I don't feel good."

"Honey, why don't you go up to my bed and lay down for a

little while?" I said. "I'll be up in a little while to check on you." With three little kids, someone was always hurt. Most of the time it was nothing. I went to look in on her and while I was watching her, I saw her face go completely white, as if the blood was draining from her. She said that her side was hurting her. That scared me a little bit. So I told our friends and family to keep the party going – we were going to run Catie to the emergency room.

We left meat sizzling on the grill and the alligator cake with the candy-corn teeth on the counter. We said, "We'll be back shortly. Just keep everything going. Hang on to the piñata, though. Catie will definitely want to take a swing at it."

Larry drove to the hospital while I sat in the back of the van with Catie. She was feeling really sick and then started vomiting.

When we got to the emergency room, we told the intake person that Catie had fallen and had thrown up in the car. They immediately sent Catie in for a CT scan. We all just sat around and waited. Larry and I were thinking that maybe she had a cracked or possibly even something more serious like an injured spleen.

I was a little anxious because it was taking so long to get the CT results. But I kept telling myself that kids get hurt all the time and it's probably nothing serious. Catie was the picture of health.

So while we waited, I was trying to mentally make a list of what I needed to do. We were planning to take a vacation the next day to a dude ranch with some good friends. I hadn't packed yet but figured I could do it when we got home. We were looking forward to our little vacation. We had saved up for it and couldn't wait to spend time with our friends.

Life was good.

Chapter 2

She's Cured

We had been at the hospital for well over three hours. Catie was in one of those bleak rooms. Gray walls and nothing fun to look at. Larry and I were with her and we kept waiting to hear from the doctor. I finally went out to the nurses' station to see what was holding us up. The nurse had a funny look on her face, like she wanted to say something but couldn't. She asked if someone had spoken to us. When I told her that no one had come to see us yet, she went and got the doctor. For the first time, fear was knotting my stomach. Maybe this wasn't something simple.

The doctor came back with Catie's scan and called us into the hallway outside of her room. The hallway was cold and dim and smelled of medicine and fear. He showed us a tumor that was growing on her kidney and adrenal gland. We were stunned and asked, "But it's not cancer, right?" When he said, "We are pretty sure that it is," our lives were forever altered. I actually felt sorry for the doctor who had to give us the news. I was sure that when he saw Catie, he thought that it would be something simple, that the cute blond-haired bubbly little girl couldn't be sick. I was pretty sure that having to tell us parents the news that our daughter had cancer totally ruined his night.

With the wall behind us holding us up, Larry and I looked at each other in disbelief. How could this be happening? Our six-year-old daughter has cancer?

We made a quick call to update my family.

"Mom, we have to go to Albany Medical Center. Catie has cancer."

"What? What are you talking about?" I could hear the tears in her voice.

"Mom, they found a tumor. We don't know what we are doing. Can you and Dad stay at the house with the boys. We don't know when we'll be home."

"Of course, honey."

Larry and I lay down with Catie in her bed and just chatted while the doctors and nurses called an ambulance to take her to Albany Medical Center. They wouldn't let me be in the back of the ambulance, but I was able to ride up in front. With lights flashing and sirens blaring, I was grateful that Catie thought it was a great adventure. The ambulance ride felt like it took forever. I would look back at Catie in the ambulance to make sure she was okay and to make sure she wasn't scared. Then I would turn around and sob quietly into my hands. The ambulance driver was trying to help me calm down and once I felt in control of myself, I would turn around to check on her again. Larry ran home to get us some clothes and make sure the boys were taken care of. He met us back in the ER at Albany Med.

Everything felt so surreal. How could we have a daughter who had cancer? We were having a birthday party. The cake was still on the counter. This could not be happening. We had to call our friends and explain that our trip was off. No vacation, just cancer.

Not one person could believe that our six-year old, bubbly, curly blond-haired, happy daughter actually had cancer. It just didn't make sense. We waited for a long time in the ER until finally she was admitted. We met a surgeon the next day. We were told that the tumor would have to be removed. Most of the doctors thought that Catie had Wilms tumor, which can be a very treatable form of pediatric cancer. We were looking at several months of chemotherapy, but all with the hopes of a cure. Everyone said that if you had to have cancer, this was the kind to have.

During a long and difficult surgery, the surgeon removed Catie's kidney and adrenal gland. When pathology came back we learned that she had neuroblastoma, a very rare and difficult cancer to treat. Larry did his research and talked to Dr. Nai Kong Cheung at Memorial Sloan-Kettering Cancer Center in New York to see what we should do next. He recommended some testing to see if the cancer had spread to her bone or bone marrow.

One of the tests that Catie needed was a bone marrow biopsy. The doctor asked us to be in the room with Catie and told us they would give her something so she wouldn't remember anything about the procedure. Then the doctor started drilling through Catie's iliac crests, those small dimples on the lower back, with something that looked like a corkscrew. She was crying and I know that it hurt a lot. I held on to her and kept talking to her, trying to distract her and keep her calm. But what I really wanted to do was reach across the table and throttle the doctor. I knew that I couldn't cry in front of Catie. But the thought that kept running through my head was, *Never again. You are kidding yourself if you think she's not going to remember this.* She remembered and I never forgot. The next time a doctor told us this procedure needed to be done, we made sure that Catie had anesthesia. And it's probably a good thing that the first doctor was not around for the second procedure, because I wanted to do a bone marrow biopsy on him – with no sedation.

Ultimately we were thrilled to learn that the cancer had not spread and that she was considered Stage 1. Stage 1 was good, very good. She didn't even need chemotherapy or radiation because the tumor was encapsulated and the surgeon got the whole thing.

The doctors at Sloan-Kettering recommended physical check ups every three months and a CT scan at the six- and 12-month marks. Catie started first grade in the fall and we all felt that we had dodged a bullet. There were times when it just felt completely unreal. I would burst out crying at odd moments and always felt like something was hanging over our heads. But with three little kids, we needed to get back to normal. I went back to volunteering in the kids' classrooms and after a few good checkups and scans, we started to relax.

One day Catie wasn't feeling well and I brought her to the pediatrician. I was frantic because all I could think about was the cancer returning. Catie was lying on the floor with her head on my lap. Tears were streaming down my face and I was absolutely petrified. Our pediatrician did a really thorough checkup and decided Catie had pneumonia, but he was still worried because of the cancer. We spent several hours at the doctor's office as he ran every test he could think of. He called the pediatric oncologist who told our pediatrician that Catie was cured, to stop looking for cancer. Wow, what a relief!

Chapter 3

It's Back

Life was moving along and we started to breathe easier once we heard the "C" word – you know, Cure. Catie loved first grade and came home happy every day from school. She was active and healthy and learning so many new things. At her first-grade presentation, where each child had to represent a person or thing, she got to be cotton candy. Her little poem was adorable, perfect for a child so sweet.

At her 12-month scan, Catie went in for in her CT scan. I was in the control room. As the technicians were scanning her, they told me they needed a few more pictures and extended the area they were scanning. My heart started to race. I knew that if they were extending the area to be scanned, they saw something. When the scan was done, the doctors told us to go home, to not worry, they would call us. Larry and I looked at them like they were crazy. I thought I knew what it meant when they had to take more pictures. I wasn't moving until we got the results. Well, the results showed that the tumor was back. Now it was in her liver, her lungs and around her spinal column. Now this was Stage IV neuroblastoma. Not good.

When we met with the doctor, he told us that he couldn't do anything for her. He basically abandoned us. He didn't refer us to another hospital or call another doctor. He just gave us the news and walked out of the room. Frightened and frantic, Larry immediately got on the phone with doctors at Sloan-Kettering and Dana Farber in Boston. Sloan-Kettering was at the forefront of the treatment, offering a decent percentage for survival. Two days later the three of us were on our way to New York to meet with Dr. Cheung.

Catie, with her usual sense of excitement, saw this as a great adventure. Before heading to the hospital, we walked around Manhattan. She was absolutely mesmerized by the sights. She had a little camera and was taking pictures of everything. You could see people on the street watching as she took her pictures, trying to figure out what she was seeing.

On our first day at the hospital, it felt like we had entered a war zone. Children in various stages of baldness, with IV's sticking out of them, were wandering around. Parents were chatting and visiting. I wanted to scream. I ended up in the bathroom about 15 times that day. I felt like I couldn't breathe. Parents were throwing about the names of protocols and chemotherapies and doctors. I felt like we had entered an alternative universe. Catie, on the other hand, was smiling and meeting other kids, bouncing around in the playroom.

When we finally met with the doctor, he told us that Catie would need to have her liver biopsied and have additional testing. Still numb and terrified, we hunkered down for the new battle. He set up the tests immediately and Catie was scheduled for surgery.

The doctors felt that Catie's disease definitely didn't follow the path of most neuroblastoma patients. Many of the children were diagnosed after months of uncertainty, with vague symptoms that could be attributed to many things. Children didn't show up at Sloan-Kettering like Catie, with smiles on their faces looking healthy and happy and exuberant. When they looked at her scans and then looked at her running around and Hula Hooping in the playroom, they said it just didn't make sense.

When pathology from the biopsy came in, Larry, Catie and I met with the doctor to go over the protocol. We were worried about how to tell Catie that she was going to have to have a port put into her chest and that she would lose her hair. The doctor explained what was going to happen, going over the chemotherapy, the surgeries and the radiation. She just nodded. I sat there, clutching Larry's hand and tried not to cry.

The doctor told Catie that the chemo would make her lose her hair. We were holding our breath wondering how she would take it, losing her gorgeous, shiny, blond curly hair. I told her we could get hats and scarves or whatever she wanted. She thought about it for a minute and then without missing a beat said, "Nah, that's okay. I'll just be bald."

The doctor smiled.

As Larry and I looked at each other with relief, we thought, *Where did we get her from?* And with that, we left the conference room and Catie went to play with her new friends.

Chapter 4

Laughter Is The Best Medicine

Most people think a closet is a place to store things or a place to hide. For Catie, a closet meant a place to explore and find delight. Even if that closet was a place in Sloan-Kettering where she was being treated for cancer. All she needed was a partner to join in the fun.

Catie began treatment and we settled into a new routine. We moved into the Ronald McDonald House, which was five blocks from the hospital, purchased a jogging stroller and got into the habit of walking back and forth each day to the clinic for chemo.

One day shortly after treatment began, Catie and I were back down in nuclear medicine for another scan when we saw a mom and her son playing cards. We introduced ourselves and chatted for a while. Lynn and Kevin were staying at the Ronald McDonald House too. Kevin had been diagnosed with neuroblastoma at the age of four. He had already been treated at several hospitals throughout the country and was being monitored by Sloan because it looked like he was relapsing.

Catie and Kevin became fast friends. Those two could be found writing books, "borrowing" medical supplies and telling the doctors what to do. They were trouble in the absolute best sense of the word. If you saw one of the kids, you knew the other one wasn't far behind.

One week, the kids were both having treatment. Kevin was having antibody therapy, which usually meant pre-medication with Benadryl and then lots of pain medication throughout the day. The treatment was not easy. Catie was on a chemotherapy that basically made her throw up for seven days straight.

That week, Catie and Kevin decided that they wanted to room together during the days of their treatment. They were eyeing a very small space with no windows. Lynn and I said "Oh no, they want the closet!"

They were put into a tiny room with two small beds in it. Usually we were out in the general clinic area with just a curtain separating the kids. But this room was more private, so Lynn and I looked at each other and said, "Go for it! Make it anything you want it to be!"

While in the "closet," Catie and Kevin worked on their book called "Doctor Destroyer." In the book, they eradicated most of the doctors and some of the assistants, like the finger-stick lady (she was the one who had to prick their fingers every day to check their blood counts). Lynn and I laughed, "Are you sure you want to kill off Dr. Cheung and keep Dr. Kushner?" We didn't always agree with their choices, but we respected their individual preferences.

Throughout the week, the kids made bets with each other over various things. The prize was usually a Snickers bar or something equally delicious and unhealthy. We would laugh and Lynn would say, "Well, there are almost 300 calories and some of it is protein!" Since the kids didn't have much of an appetite,

Lynn would cheer on Kevin and I would cheer on Catie. When 300 calories are on the line, the prize probably meant more to me and Lynn than to the kids.

Catie and Kevin decided to make a fort in the "closet" with sheets and blankets. "Mom, you and Lynn have to guard the door until we are ready to let the nurses and doctors in!" The room was tiny, crowded with two small crib-like cots and several IV poles. Lynn and I had to move the two chairs into the hallway to make a little more room. The kids started with a pile of sheets and blankets, first draping the sheets over the sides of the beds. Then they started working on covering every part of their room, with the IV poles marking the small passageway to their beds. The kids were not visible from the doorway, but we could hear them chatting and laughing.

Entering the room meant stooping over and carefully working your way through the coverings to get to the kids. This was no easy task for the nurses and doctors as they came in balancing chemo bags, IV drugs and medical orders. I wondered if they were going to get annoyed with Catie and Kevin. But I should have known better. They just took it in stride, not even flinching. The kids spent that whole week laughing, plotting and playing.

At one point I asked her doctor, after he climbed through the maze of their little room, "Are you sure there is chemo in Catie's IV?"

He looked at me alarmed and said "Why are you asking me this?"

"Well, Catie hasn't thrown up all day and Kevin didn't need pain medication," I said. He reviewed the chemo order and what was written on the bag with a worried look. "No, she is getting the chemo. I don't know what's going on."

I said, "Look at the kids!"

With a huge grin on his face, he saw their smiles and heard their giggling. Shaking his head in amazement, he said, "Laughter is absolutely the best medicine!"

Chapter 5

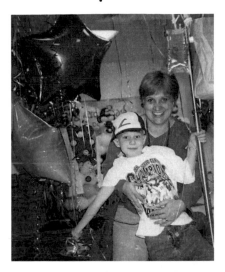

Teach Your Parents Well

When we first went to Sloan-Kettering, I was in a state of disbelief. I wanted everyone to feel badly that we had a daughter with cancer. I couldn't understand how life was just moving on when my daughter was sick. Rather than feeling sorry for myself, I should have been watching Catie. She went about her days doing what she could and didn't let anyone's comments faze her.

After she started chemotherapy, Larry and I tried to get Catie's hair cut short so it wouldn't be as hard for her when it started to fall out. We stopped by a local salon and asked how much it would be to clip her hair. When the hairdresser said $25, I wanted to shake her and say, *Are you kidding me – this kid is going to lose her hair because of cancer and you want $25 for a two minute trim?* I don't know why I expected everyone to come to our aid, but I did. But Catie said, "That's okay, Mom."

Shortly after this, we took Catie to a pizzeria around the corner from the Ronald McDonald House. I was watching a father and his son eat and play. The boy was maybe four years old with a bunch of auburn curls. I watched them laughing and talking and playing. All I could think of is, *Lucky you. Living your carefree life with your healthy kid. If you only knew how lucky you are!* But I was the one who didn't know anything because two days later I saw the same father and son at Sloan-Kettering. When I approached them to say hello, I learned that the little boy had retinoblastoma and was probably going to lose his eye. I didn't like myself very much that day, but boy did I learn a lesson.

I still had a lot to learn. Another time I was taking Catie out for a walk. She was in the jogging stroller and I was pushing her along on the Upper East Side of Manhattan. We had had a long day of chemotherapy at the hospital and I wanted to buy her a treat. We went into one of Catie's favorite stores, a small electronics store, and were looking around for Nintendo games. A woman looked at Catie and said, "Aren't you a little old to be in a stroller? You should give your mom a break."

I fought the urge to smack this woman. I snapped, "Well she had a long day of chemotherapy, so I guess she's earned the right to ride."

Catie just smiled and said, "We're looking for a video game." The woman looked abashed. I wished I handled the situation a little more gracefully. Somewhere inside of me was a courteous and dignified mom who could respond to these statements with grace. I just couldn't seem to locate her.

Thank God we have kids around to teach us lessons.

Catie and I were home for a visit and I had taken a group of kids to the local ice cream store. The kids were ordering their goodies.

"I want mint chocolate chip," sang out one of the kids.

Another one piped up with, "I'll take a hot fudge sundae."

The man behind the counter was taking the orders and he pointed at Catie, asking, "And what would he like?"

I responded, "She would like butter pecan."

He said again, " No, him," pointing at Catie.

Once again, glaring at him, I said "she" with a slow, simmering anger. When he said it the third time, I refrained from whacking him, but just barely. I really wanted to beat the crap out of him.

Robby, listening to this exchange, turned to the man and matter of factly said, "Oh, that's my sister. She doesn't have hair because she has cancer."

Catie just smiled and said, "I'd really like butter pecan, please!"

Ah, so that's how it's done. Who knew that my six-year-old son and seven-year-old daughter would be teaching me how to respond to these situations that made my blood boil. Thank you, Robby. Thank you, Catie. Maybe there is a way to find that grace and dignity within me. I just have to listen to my kids.

Chapter 6

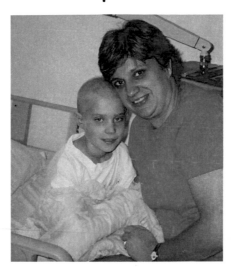

A Day In The Life

Life as a cancer mom was exhausting, not just physically, but mentally and emotionally. I wanted to stay as calm and upbeat as possible around Catie, but there were times when the anxiety of her disease got the better of me. Sleep was very hard to come by. But during those long days at the hospital, I watched as Catie handled her treatment with her usual nonchalance. No drama, no crying. Just dealing with it. And I knew that I could learn from her.

Oh, my God. Is it 7 o'clock already? I had found myself awake in the middle of the night, once again, unable to sleep, consumed with worry. I kept thinking there was some magical cure around the corner, if only I could just find it. What I found was that I was always exhausted.

I took a quick peek at Catie to make sure she was okay and then I hopped into the shower to begin another day as a cancer mom. As I toweled off, I mentally checked off the things we needed to bring with us. Catie would need her vomit basin and a box of tissues along with a warm sweatshirt, a blanket, snacks and something fun to do. I would need my pocketbook and our hospital bag, containing the binder with all of the important papers and reports related to Catie's treatment.

"Good morning, sunshine," I said to wake her. She smiled up at me and climbed out of bed. We decided what would be comfortable to wear – something easily accessible for IV lines and something warm enough for a skinny little body. Once she was dressed, she crawled into the jogging stroller (one of the best purchases we ever made). I slung our bag over the handles. I wheeled her to the elevator at the Ronald McDonald House. We lived on the 10th floor at the end of the hallway. As we headed out of the house, we decided to turn right so that we could travel down First Avenue because that is where the good coffee shop was.

We walked from 72nd Street down to 70th. where I struggled to get the stroller through the door of Timothy's Coffee. I grabbed a large, strong cup and a muffin and I got Catie a donut. When we got to 68th Street, we turned left so that we could go into the side entrance for Sloan-Kettering. This was the easiest entrance to get into with a stroller. There were no steps or escalators to navigate and the door opened automatically. We headed to the elevator right around the corner.

Once we got up to the seventh-floor clinic, we checked in. Today was going to be a long day – 12 hours of chemotherapy. Catie got her counts checked by the "finger-stick lady" and when she was done we headed to the back of the clinic to grab a bed. A large room was separated by curtains and there were about 20 beds for kids there. We said hi to our friends and settled in for the day.

Catie's nurse, Kateri, came by with Catie's chemo and hooked her up. Catie settled down, hoping that today would be a good day. As I sat next to her bed, we talked or played games or painted our nails. We had to be careful with the nails because the smell of the polish could bother some of the other kids. We always asked to make sure it was okay.

Catie dozed off for a while and I sat in the chair next to her bed. I was so tired that I couldn't really think straight and couldn't remember the last time I slept the whole night through. I took out my binder and marked down Catie's chemo and blood counts. It gave me a tiny sense of control to keep track of these things. While she was sleeping, I took a minute to check on John, Simon, Sebastian, Breanna, Allie and Kevin. These kids were our friends. They all had neuroblastoma. Their moms and I were friends, too.

I headed back to Catie's bed and sat down, trying to relax a little. When Catie started to feel nauseous, I got Kateri and we started with one of the anti-emetic drugs, hoping it would keep her from vomiting. We had to try several of these drugs until we found the combination that seemed to give Catie some relief.

Some of the other kids stopped by with their parents and we chatted if Catie was awake. If not, I would slip over to some of the moms and we shared a few moments of chitchat – "How did the scans go? Did John have his surgery? How did Simon make out with the hot antibodies?" We parents were a solid group. We looked out for each other.

At lunchtime, the cafeteria cart was brought up to the floor. Catie wasn't hungry at all, but I grabbed a half of a tuna sandwich and a banana. I was so grateful that the hospital sent this cart up for us because it meant we didn't have to leave our kids to get food. I settled back in to my chair next to Catie's bed and tried to get comfortable. It seemed that every time I start to doze off, Catie needed something. So, although all I did was sit around and watch her, I was exhausted. I had nothing to show for all this time. It amazed me how little I was able to accomplish during so many hours at the hospital.

Around 2:15 I saw that Catie was sound asleep. I looked over at Lynn and asked, "Do you want a coffee from the cart? I am going to run down."

She said, "That would be great. Make it a large with a little cream."

I took the stairs down to the first floor. The elevator was too slow and the Starbucks cart closed at 2:30. As I skidded to a stop in the line for coffee, the man who served us asked me, "Do you work here? I see you all the time."

"No, my daughter is being treated here."

"Well, I think that earns you the employee discount," he said with a smile.

As I thanked him, I was once again touched by the small moments of kindness that surrounded us here in this amazing hospital. I took the elevator back up, afraid that the coffee would end up all over me if I took the stairs. Also, I just didn't feel like walking up seven flights. I handed Lynn her coffee and took my seat next to Catie.

Dinnertime rolled around. I asked, "Catie, do you think you can eat anything?"

When she said, "I think I want Chinese," I knew what this meant. I asked Lynn to keep an eye on her for a few minutes as I headed down stairs and ran across the street. I ordered her baby corn with garlic sauce and several fortune cookies. I got the Szechuan chicken and headed back up to the clinic. We knew that at 6 o'clock we were going to be sent down to urgent care. After we ate, we headed down to the first floor and tried to grab a comfortable spot for Catie to rest. Her chemo needed to run until 9 p.m. When she fell asleep on a couch, I put my head back and dozed for a few minutes. Then I stepped away and called home to check on Larry and the boys. Catie and I missed them so much. There were so many things happening at home and we were not a part of them. Larry was happy to hear from me, but he sounded so tired. He was getting up early every day, getting the kids up, going to work, coming home, fixing them dinner and taking them to soccer and baseball and all their other activities. We both were doing our best and grateful we had each other.

When Catie's chemo buzzed at 9 o'clock, I notified one of the nurses who came over and unhooked her from the IV line. Catie sleepily crawled back into the jogging stroller and I wheeled her out the side door of the hospital. We made the return trek up York Avenue because we were in a different part of the hospital that night. We turned on 73rd Street to go to the Ronald McDonald House.

Even though we were so tired, we stopped to check on messages. "Catie, you've got a bunch of mail today," said Sue. "I don't know of anyone else who gets as much mail as you do." Catie and I smiled and headed to the elevators, wondering what she received.

When we got to our room, Catie put on her jammies and we opened the mail. As always, the letters and packages lifted our spirits. We then had to watch the Brady Bunch, just as we did every night. "Marcia, Marcia, Marcia!"

When the show was over, I gave her a goodnight kiss and said, "I love you, Catie."

I brushed my teeth and put on my pajamas. I climbed into bed next to her. We had moved the two single beds together so we could sleep next to each other. We covered the garish orange, brown and yellow bedspread with handmade quilts that were sent to us from friends. I put my head on the pillow and tried to turn my mind off. I knew I needed to sleep because we were going to have another day just like this one ahead of us the next day.

As I looked at Catie's beautiful face, sleeping so soundly, I saw a tear run down her cheek. And as I wiped it away, my eyes filling with my own tears, I thought how amazing she was. Catie didn't complain or cry or make a fuss. She took everything in stride – better than I did. People asked me where I got the strength to fight this battle. I would point to Catie and say, "Right there."

Chapter 7

The Kindness Of Strangers

In the midst of Catie's exhausting, grueling treatment, it amazed me where we found unexpected bright spots. Those times when we realized that we were not alone, that people are good, that the sight of a cute little girl with no hair and a bright smile can bring out the best in others.

"Mom, do we really get to go home today?" Catie asked, bouncing with excitement.

"Yup," I said. "We are finally free and we get to go home for the weekend." We had been at Sloan-Kettering since July. It was now October. After several rounds of chemo, we were heading home for Catie's first visit.

Catie was so excited, but her strength hadn't caught up with her enthusiasm. She had lost about 10 pounds since treatment started (and she was slim to start with) and the chemo had zapped her energy. But it couldn't zap her spirit. Or her smile.

That morning I had run back to the Ronald McDonald House to settle our bill for the past three months. We were still residents there, but before we left I wanted to make sure we were paid up. At $20 a night, the House was a huge bargain for New York City, but it still meant $600 a month when you were living there. As Sue at the desk looked at our account, she said, "You are all paid up."

"No, we're not. We haven't paid since the first week."

"Well, you have an anonymous donor who has paid your bill, so you are all set."

"Can you please tell me who it is?" I begged.

"Nope" she said. "Go home and enjoy the weekend."

I ran back to Sloan-Kettering with tears in my eyes. I silently thanked the person who paid our bill. When I got to the hospital, Catie was ready and waiting. We grabbed a cab to Penn Station and I got a wheelchair to bring her to the train. I had snatched a bed sheet from the hospital to put over the train seat because her counts were still low, which meant that she was very susceptible to infection.

We had time to get a slice of pizza before our train was due to arrive. Catie looked frail and had already lost her hair, so it was obvious that she was sick. But her smile and her happiness were very much in evidence. As we sat near the Pizza Hut, we discussed the beanie babies we wanted to get.

There was a snowman Beanie Baby that was just calling to her. It was not a new one; it had been retired, so it cost more than the other Beanies. We spotted one at the kiosk in Penn Station but it was $40, a little too steep for a beanbag. "Mom, I know it's too expensive, but isn't he so cute?"

"He is really cute, honey, but we can't spend $40 on a Beanie Baby."

"I know, Mom, but he is so cute!"

As we were talking we noticed a gentleman go up to the kiosk and buy the snowman. He had been sitting near us and I had seen him glance at Catie a few times. Catie and I looked at each other.

"Oh, wow, he bought the snowman," Catie said.

"I know, honey. We'll keep looking for a snowman that is a little more reasonable."

A moment later, the man approached our table. He handed Catie the snowman. She looked at him with a huge smile and said, "Thank you, thank you, thank you. Why are you giving this to me?"

He said with tears in his eyes "This means so much to you and I want you to have it. Enjoy your visit home." So this man, this stranger, had overheard our conversation and knew that Catie was getting to go home for the first time in months. And he knew that she really wanted that Beanie Baby.

When I asked him for his name and address to thank him, he said, "Have a wonderful visit at home. That's more than enough thanks."

As Catie again said, "Thank you, thank you so much," and she turned to look at me. "Can you believe he did such a nice thing? Mom, why are you crying? "

A few minutes later we headed to the gate for our train to Albany. Catie was all bundled up, clutching her new snowman. We settled into two seats facing each other so we had lots of room. I had spread the sheet all over Catie's side so that she could stretch out. Her little bald head was peeking out from the sheet along with that smile of hers.

As the conductor came by, I handed him our tickets. Catie said, "We're going to go home. I haven't been home in almost three months!" He looked at me, he looked at Catie, he looked at Catie's bald little head and pale complexion, he looked at the tickets, and then he handed the tickets back to me. "You don't need these today."

Somehow Catie's spirit managed to shine through. She touched everyone around her. Family, friends and strangers all wanted to see Catie smile. At the end of several rounds of high dose chemotherapy at Sloan-Kettering, looking at just a few days home, I was touched by the kindness and generosity that seemed to surround us.

Chapter 8

Play Time

The playroom at Sloan-Kettering performs a very important role for the kids in treatment. It is a social center, a learning place, a place to have fun and to have celebrations. Games, movies, birthday parties, the prom – it has it all. It is staffed by Child-Life Specialists and volunteers. And Catie loved all of it. Whether it was the daily craft, Bingo, a party or just watching a movie, it was one of our favorite places. The kids got to be kids for a little while, just hanging out in the playroom. Catie was a master at enjoying herself and getting other kids to have fun.

The Child Life Specialist at Sloan-Kettering was unassuming. But for a little person, Trish packed a big punch. She was under 5 feet tall with straight brown hair, bright eyes, a big smile and freckles. The warmth of her personality could melt a glacier. From the minute we met her, we knew she was someone special. Somehow she managed to reach every child in treatment. And there was a wide variety of personalities for her to deal with.

When Catie and Kevin started their first book, <u>Doctor Destroyer</u>, Trish made sure they kept working on it until it was finished. She managed to procure very large blank journals and provided the kids with pencils and markers. She also made sure that there was a new craft every day for the kids and parents to work on.

Her compassion was endless. When Lizzie, one of the kids who was battling leukemia, was leaving to go home, with no further treatment options, Trish went around with a Polaroid camera and took pictures of all of Lizzie's friends, nurses and doctors. Lizzie and her mom went home with a memory book of their time in New York.

At one point things were not going well with Catie's treatment. Catie had relapsed off of the N7 protocol and no child had ever survived a relapse. We knew our options were limited and we knew we had to make the most of the time we had together. We were heading home for a long weekend when Trish came up to me and said "How would you guys like to spend the weekend at Lake Placid? I have it all set up."

"What? Trish, that sounds awesome. Thank you so much."

So Larry, the three kids and I headed to Lake Placid where Trish had made arrangements for us to stay in a hotel owned by one of her friends.

"Mom, can we go up the gondola?" Catie asked.

"Sure honey" I said in a wavery voice. I am not a big fan of heights and the thought of hanging a hundred feet in the air in an open swing did not thrill me. But all three kids wanted to go. As I sat next to Catie, our feet dangling, she chatted away.

"Hey Mom, look. If we swing our feet we can make the gondola swing high." *Great – just what I need.*

When we got to the Olympic arena, the kids got their picture taken standing in First, Second and Third Place. They loved the medals they received.

Back at the hotel was an outdoor pool. Now this was late fall.

The weather was not really warm and the water in the pool felt like recently melted ice cubes. So we told the kids "The first one in gets a dollar." Johnny, who was four at the time, dove right in. Catie followed right behind and Robby behind her. There was no way that Larry and I were going in. That pool was freezing. But it was well worth the dollar to see their happy, but cold, faces.

We ended up meeting Trish's friends. The woman said to me "Your daughter must be very special because Trish has never, ever done this for anyone. " Trish had given us a vacation – a vacation from the hospital, from chemo, from stress, from work, from fear.

When we got back to our room, the boys fell asleep on the bunk beds and Catie was curled up on the couch in her new navy blue fleece vest and skirt, with her little Timberland boots hanging over the side. She picked up a chapter book and started reading. Larry and I loved reading to the kids, but we weren't sure any of them inherited our love of reading. We smiled at each other as we watched Catie, absorbed in her book. It was a gift to us, another milestone we got to enjoy.

Being a volunteer at the Sloan-Kettering playroom was quite an honor. They had a long waiting list of people wishing to volunteer there. The people that we got to know changed the way we looked at hospitals.

Right toward the beginning of Catie's treatment she was diagnosed with C-diff. It is a bacterium in your intestines and is very contagious and causes diarrhea. So when Catie was in-patient, she had to be in isolation. The upside was we got our own room. The downside was that she couldn't go to the playroom. But we didn't let that stop us. Every day I would trek to the playroom, get the day's craft, and then grab some supplies for our own projects. Our room was always covered in glitter, glue, crepe paper and construction paper.

Friday night was Bingo night and all of the in-patient kids really looked forward to it. The volunteers made sure that each child went back to the room with a prize. Because Catie was in isolation, she couldn't participate. One of the first Fridays that we couldn't go to Bingo, we heard a knock on our door.

"Come on in" Catie yelled.

There stood one of the playroom volunteers, John, with a Bingo set in his hands. Alongside of him was another volunteer. They handed us our Bingo boards and Isolation Bingo was born! They stood at Catie's door and called out the numbers so we could play. Every Friday that Catie was in isolation he would come to our room. Catie was thrilled to be able to play. As an aside, we parents always loved it when B9 was called. (Benign – get it?)

One day as John and I were chatting, he said "I just want you to know that I am going to go to medical school and your daughter is one of the main reasons I am going. How she can keep that smile on her face just amazes me. She is absolutely an inspiration."

"John, wow. I am so impressed and I know you'll make a great doctor. Your compassion shines through every day. Thank you for making Catie a part of your decision."

Catie loved to keep busy. At one point she was making bracelets out of embroidery yarn. All of the nurses loved them so one of the playroom volunteers encouraged Catie to start selling them. Catie would sit there on her hospital bed, bright strands of thread surrounding her and with a smile on her face she went to work.

"Catie, how much are you selling the bracelets for?" asked one of the nurses.

"I don't know, I was thinking about a dollar."

The volunteer piped in "Hey this is Manhattan, you better charge three bucks for those."

Catie grinned and said "Do you really think people will pay $3 for these? Mom, let's get working!" And so we did.

Some of the volunteers would meet us out for dinner (which I think was against the rules.) We talked about love lives and school and family and friends. They loved to watch Catie eating her three chicken wings and drinking her milk while we adults had a beer.

I don't know what we would have done without our playroom people. They changed the way we looked at the hospital, and I like to think that maybe Catie changed the way they looked at life.

Chapter 9

Happy Halloween

Catie loved holidays. Any holiday. But Halloween was really special because she loved to dress up and go trick or treating and eat candy. She wasn't going to let something like cancer get in her way. Larry and I didn't want her to miss out on any of it. With her chemo schedule, we were pretty sure that she was going to be in-patient on October 31st.

"Mom, I really want to be Tweety Bird this year," Catie said.

"Well, honey, I'm not sure where we can get a Tweety costume," I said. "But we can try."

I should have known better. Larry, who was in New York for a visit with us said, "I have an errand to run. I'll be back soon." When he got back, he arrived with a beautiful, fuzzy, warm head-to-toe Tweety costume from the Warner Bros. store. He looked at me and said, "Don't ask how much it cost."

"Wow, Dad. You did it. Can I wear it to the Halloween party

in the playroom? If we make it home before Halloween, can I show my friends?"

"Of course, honey, that's why we got it," Larry said.

Well, we made it home a week before Halloween and decided to throw a last-minute party. We invited all of Catie's friends from school. Robby and Johnny's friends were there too. Catie wore her Tweety costume and looked so happy, running around, visiting with her friends. I was just grateful it was warm.

As I watched all of the kids running around, I kept asking my friends, "Doesn't Catie look good?"

There was my seven year-old-girl, about 10 pounds thinner, bald and with a runny nose running around with a huge grin in a Tweety costume. I know I was trying to convince myself that Catie looked just like the other kids. The other parents smiled and said, "Yeah, she looks great." But I knew she didn't.

That Sunday Catie and I had to head back to New York. She was scheduled for more chemotherapy. We knew we wouldn't make it home for the actual day of Halloween.

The playroom at Sloan-Kettering threw the best parties. The social workers and child-life specialists knew how important it was for the kids to have something to look forward to, something fun, hopefully involving candy. The Halloween party was scheduled for the Friday of that week.

"Mom, the playroom is having a Halloween party. Can we go?"

"Of course, honey, we wouldn't miss it."

"I think Kevin is going to be here for the party. I wonder what he is going to be."

The day of the party she was jumping with excitement. Kevin, all dressed up with a hiking vest and hat, toting a fake gun, was waiting for us. He was Indiana Jones. When he saw Catie dressed as Tweety Bird, he said, "I think I'm going bird hunting."

The next day, Catie was admitted to the hospital because her counts were so low and she had a fever. Sunday was Halloween. And we really wanted to make the day special. Larry came down to visit for the day. Catie was supposed to stay in her hospital room because her counts were so low, which meant that she was at risk for an infection. But there was no way we were keeping her in that hospital room. That wasn't going to happen on Halloween.

As we snuck Catie out of her room with her Tweety costume on and a mask covering her mouth and nose, we trekked around the public areas of the hospital, trick or treating. Catie didn't know that Larry ran ahead and gave candy to the nurses so that when we got to them, they could fill Catie's Halloween bag. We saw more than one nurse glance at us and shake their heads as if to scold us for getting her out of her room. But those same nurses, without saying a word to us, then smiled and turned their backs so we didn't get busted.

Even the head nurse spotted us. "What are you doing out of your room?"

"Trick or treating, of course," said Catie.

"Well, I am going to pretend I didn't see you. Have fun."

As we headed back to the room, Catie said, "I can't believe all those nurses had candy for me. That was awesome."

"Yes it was, Cate." And Larry and I looked at each other and smiled, so glad that we had this day. We realized that sometimes breaking the rules is the right thing to do. Just don't tell the doctors and nurses we said so.

Chapter 10

Heaven's Helpers

The nurses and social workers at Sloan-Kettering have a special place in heaven. Throughout Catie's treatment, we were so grateful to have these people in our lives. They reached out to us, watched out for us, broke rules for us, made us laugh and made an intolerable situation not only tolerable, but also fun.

When we first went to Sloan, Larry's work gave him the freedom to be with us in New York without having to worry about his job. His boss, without hesitating, said, "Go do what you have to do. Your job will be waiting for you." After we had been down there for three weeks, Larry needed to go home, get back to work and take care of the boys. It was now up to me to take care of Catie. I was a little nervous about all of the details. There were so many things to keep track of and monitor. And I needed to make sure that Catie was happy.

The social workers held a caregiver support meeting once a

week. The problem was that I hadn't left Catie's side and she didn't want me to. But I really felt that I needed this one hour break to connect with some other adults and share my fears. We absolutely did not want the kids to see how frightened we were.

"Hey Catie, there is a parent group meeting in the playroom today for an hour. What would you think about me going to it?"

As she was saying, "Mom, I don't want to be alone. Please don't go," our nurse Kevin came into the room.

He took a look at us and said to me, "Gina, go to the meeting. I will watch Catie. You're right around the corner if we need you."

I hesitated looking at Catie's little face. I didn't think I could leave her. Kevin said, "Go, get out of here."

Catie reluctantly agreed.

I went to the meeting and the discussion centered on being able to take time to take care of ourselves. I said, "I totally agree, but what do you do when your kid doesn't want you to leave?" We all kind of laughed at the dilemma. I spent the whole hour worrying about Catie. *Was she sad, was she crying, did she need me?*

As I hurried back to the room at the end of the hour, I heard Catie chattering away. On her lap was a cloth doll and beside her bed was a medical kit.

"Hi Mom. How was the meeting?"

"It was fine honey. What did you do?"

"Well, Kevin came in with this doll and told me that I could do surgery. So I put in a broviac so the doll could get medicine just like me. (A broviac is a port inserted into the chest with tubes coming out of it. This allows doctors and nurses to give meds and draw blood without having to use a needle.) Look, he even showed me how to use the betadine to clean the spot before the surgery."

Kevin came to the door and smiled. "She did great. I hope you enjoyed the meeting."

"Kevin, I don't know how to thank you."

"My pleasure," he replied.

One of Catie's favorite treats was the pretzels from Auntie Anne's. The problem was the only place in New York City that had them was in Penn Station. Even if I hopped into a cab, I would have been gone for well over an hour. That wasn't going to happen. One Friday night as Kevin was leaving, he said, "I'll see you later."

I remember thinking, *You mean we will see you next week.* About an hour later Kevin showed up in Catie's room with two plain pretzels frosted with the glaze that Catie loved. Kevin lived in New Jersey. He had driven across town to Penn Station, ran in and got the pretzels, hopped back in the car and drove back to the hospital to deliver the pretzels to Catie. All on a Friday night. How do you thank someone for that? Catie was beyond thrilled.

Joan, a nurse practitioner, really hit it off with Catie. The three of us would discuss Joan's love life, who she was meeting, where, when, how did it go? I guess Catie got her desire to be a matchmaker from me. She and Joan would also talk a lot about the Yankees. It was a well-known fact that Joan was a huge Yankee fan. Her lab coat was covered with Yankee pins. And Joan made it clear to all that she was not giving them away. Never. Not one. Except to Catie, who got the one pin she truly coveted. Catie was so excited, bubbling over. But Catie had to promise not to tell anyone that Joan had given it to her.

One time after Catie had been in-patient for quite a while, it looked like we wouldn't make it home for Christmas. Catie had a fever and the doctors were trying to figure out which antibiotic would work best. They had her on one that could affect her hearing. Catie already had hearing loss because of the chemo, but for some reason, the thought of this antibiotic taking away more of her hearing was killing me. When I learned she still needed to be on it, I walked into the hallway and just started sobbing. Joan came up to me and asked, "What's wrong, Gina?"

"Joan, she still has to be on the Gentamycin. I can't stand that she will lose more of her hearing. And now it looks like we won't make it home for Christmas."

Joan walked into the room, changed the order, came out and said, "This other antibiotic will do just fine." I hugged her and thanked her many times and then went back into the room to be with Catie.

I remember so many times when our nurses held my hands, comforted me, walked with me, helped me get my bearings. I remember the times that they spent with Catie, taking care of her, making her feel special. These people, who went above and beyond, touched our lives in so many ways. To us they were gifts from heaven. The nurses and social workers made us feel special, cared for, loved. We loved them right back. Big time!

Chapter 11

It Takes A Village

I don't know what we would have done without our friends. When we went to New York they immediately stepped in and did whatever was needed. A rotation of meals was set up so that Larry and the boys could have a nice dinner several times a week. Rides were offered, playdates were scheduled, cards were sent, and packages were mailed to the Ronald McDonald House.

One thing that impressed me was their ability to just "do something." They didn't wait around to be told what to do. They just did something. Our church organized fundraisers for us. My family in Batavia set up coin jars in local restaurants to help defray the cost of treatment. And locally, our friends were figuring out what to do.

One day I got a call from my friend Nancy. "Hey Gina, Andrea wants to organize a fundraiser. A Beanie Baby sale. What do you think?"

"I think it sounds fantastic! (This was at the height of the Beanie Baby craze.) I think it's a perfect fundraiser for Catie. Do you remember the day she relapsed? She was laying on the floor in the family surrounded by her beanies. Please tell Andrea I think it's a great idea and thank her for me."

So while I was in New York with Catie, our friends were doing their planning in Clifton Park. Catie's friends not only donated Beanie Babies for the event, but then they went to the fundraiser and bought other ones.

When we made it home for Christmas, Andrea called and asked if she could stop by. She wanted to tell us about the event. I had heard that it was a success so I thought that maybe they raised $500 or $600. When Andrea came in, she had a laundry basket filled with gift cards to local restaurants, snacks and toys. It was awesome. And then she handed me a check. A check in the amount of $10,000!

"Oh my God, Andrea. Are you kidding? This is beyond generous!" And I started to cry.

"Gina, people were more than happy to be a part of this. We want you to take this money and have fun with Catie. We know how expensive New York City can be, so we want you to enjoy your time with her."

I was stunned. Because of our friends, we were able to go places and do things that we would not have been able to do without their support. I knew that our friends meant it, that they wanted Catie to have whatever fun she could. And she did.

Because of our friends' generosity, Catie became a regular at Benihana's, a Japanese steakhouse. The staff would start smiling the minute we walked in the door. The hostess would ask Catie, "Do you have your barbecue sauce?" because Catie always brought in her own Kraft barbecue sauce to have with her chicken.

FAO Schwarz toy store was one of our favorite places when people came to visit. Catie loved showing her friends around the place. And there was always the Museum of Natural History and the Little Shop of Plaster. We had so much fun that, at times, it was strange to think that Catie was in treatment for cancer.

We often went out to dinner or got takeout to eat at the Ronald McDonald House or the hospital. The generous donations from our friends and family meant that I could take Catie wherever she wanted to go.

At one point she got hooked on chicken wings. "Mom, can we go to that place on First Avenue? Someone was telling me they have great wings." That place was a bar up the street from the Ronald McDonald House. Any misgivings I had about bringing her there were quickly forgotten when I saw how much the staff took to Catie.

"Young lady, what would you like?" the waiter would ask.

"I'd like chicken wings." Catie said.

"Okay, do you want 12 or 24?"

"Uh-oh Mom. I think I can only eat about three of them."

I don't know how she did it, but she charmed the waiters. They would see us coming and put up an order of three chicken wings. Yes, just three. And she would want a glass of milk with that. Kind of hard to find in a bar. So one of the waiters would go next door to the deli and get a quart of milk for her. Her pleasure in eating her three wings and drinking glass after glass of milk brought a smile, not only to my face, but also to that of the waiters and bartenders.

Our friends made evenings like this possible. Manhattan is a very expensive place. Their generosity allowed us to eat at new restaurants and go to fun places.

We knew how lucky we were. We knew that because of our friends, Catie was really able to take a break from treatment. Our friends were thrilled that we were able to have fun. And it wasn't just me and Catie. It also meant that when we went home, we could go to the movies or McDonald's or Jeepers, an indoor playland, with Catie's buddies.

Because of the kindness of those among us, Catie was able to have lots of fun while she was in treatment. What our friends really gave us was the ability to make the most of each day. And more importantly, the ability to make wonderful new memories. And for that, we were grateful every day.

Chapter 12

Looking On The Bright Side

Having a child in treatment means learning to roll with the punches. Just when I thought I had a handle on the calendar, the schedule would change. Sometimes it meant more chemo or another scan. Once it was even a new surgery. Catie didn't let any of that bother her. She could take an ordinary day and turn it into an adventure. More chemo meant more time with her friends in the clinic. Another scan meant playing games down in nuclear medicine. Throw in a friend or two and she had a celebration going on. As for a new surgery, well, she had that covered.

"Gina, it's Dr. Kramer. We just got a look at Catie's CT and we think she needs another thoracotomy. It looks like someone threw a handful of pebbles into her lungs. So instead of another round of chemo, we are going to do a PET scan tomorrow and then surgery on Thursday." *Crap, crap, crap. This was not good.*

Catie and I were in the car on the way to the train station

when I got the call. One of her best friends, Ashley, was with us and now we had to scramble to change plans. We were supposed to go down for only a few, so the three of us were traveling together. We had planned a few special days of Catie's favorite things to share with her best friend when we didn't have to be at the hospital. Ashley was just nine at the time. There was no way she could travel on her own.

"Hi Melanie, it's Gina. I was wondering when you were heading back home this week."

"Hey Gina. I'm taking the train back to Albany on Thursday. Why? What's up?"

Melanie was a nurse at Sloan-Kettering who happened to live nearby us in Clifton Park. She commuted down and back each week, staying usually from Monday to Thursday in the city.

"I was wondering if there was any way Ashley could ride the train back with you on Thursday. Catie now needs to have another surgery and we have Ashley with us," I said.

"Absolutely. Don't worry about a thing. We will get in touch when you get here."

I called Ashley's mom, Nancy, and explained what was going on. She talked to Ashley and we all agreed to the plan, even though Ash was a little nervous. But Catie and Ashley were so excited to spend some time together that Ashley didn't worry about her train ride home and Catie didn't worry about her surgery.

On the train, we talked about what we were going to do. "Ashley, we are definitely going to FAO Schwarz – you won't believe this place. It's the best toy store ever!"

"Okay Catie. You're the boss!"

"And we are going to eat at Benihana's, right, Mom?"

"You got that right. You have to show Ashley how much fun that place is."

So once we dropped our bags at the Ronald McDonald House, we were off. As usual, Catie was bubbling over with excitement at being able to show one of her best friends some of her favorite things in New York. Ashley, grinning from ear to ear, followed along happily. As we were hopping across a very busy Second Avenue, dodging the traffic whizzing by, Catie looked at me and said, "Mom, it's just like the game Frogger."

The next day Catie was scheduled for a PET scan. She wasn't allowed to eat before the scan because the scan metabolized glucose. We all went hungry that morning. As Catie's IV was hooked up, she and Ashley sat side by side on the hospital bed playing cards. You would have thought it was a regular playdate, except for the fact that we were in a cancer center and Catie was bald and hooked up to an IV.

I knew that Catie was really hungry, so right after the injection was completed, I approached one of our favorite nurses. "Kateri, is there any way Catie could have something to eat? She has already been injected and she's really hungry." Kateri came through with graham crackers and juice.

While Catie was having the PET, Ashley and I were not allowed in the room. We ran and got something to eat and were waiting for Catie when she came out of the nuclear medicine scan room. Then as soon as she was done, we were off. FAO Schwarz – watch out! Ashley couldn't believe that a store could be so big and have so many toys. When the toy soldiers opened the doors for the kids, they were thrilled.

Knowing that Catie's cancer was in her lungs was breaking my heart. But there was no way that was going to interfere with this visit. When the news is bad, the only cure is mani-pedis. The three of us headed to a nearby salon. For their manicures the kids chose purple, and for the pedicures they got electric blue. They were laughing and chatting the whole time.

The next morning I handed Ashley off to Melanie and they headed for Penn Station. Catie and I were waiting in the clinic for her name to be called for surgery. Larry was on a train at that time to be there when Catie got out of surgery. Once again she was not allowed to eat because of the anesthesia. I had to beg her to at least let me have a cup of coffee. She took pity on me. "Okay Mom, but just one cup. You know I can't eat anything either!"

While Catie was in surgery, Larry arrived. We waited in the open lobby area. Periodically a nurse would come around and update us. After about three hours we were told that the surgery was done and that we could see her in about a half hour.

When they finally called us in, I heard her little voice moaning, "Mommy, I want my Mommy." I ran into the room. "Hi honey. Mommy is right here. I love you."

As soon as she realized I was there, she started moaning, "I want Daddy. Where is Daddy?"

Of course Larry was right behind me and he said, "Hi Deedeedog. Daddy is right here too. I love you so much."

When she realized we were both there, she then started moaning, "I want puffed rice." We started laughing at that. The nurse said, "There is no way she can have cereal. I know the surgeon won't allow it. It will just make her throw up."

But Catie was insistent. "I want puffed rice. I want puffed rice and I know I won't throw it up."

We didn't know what to do until the surgeon came in.

"Hi Dr. Laquaglia. There's our girl and guess what – she wants puffed rice."

He grinned and said, "So what are you waiting for? Get her the puffed rice."

Larry was out the door in a flash. He ran the five blocks to Gristedes and came back with a box of puffed rice and milk. The nurses didn't look too pleased, but hey, Dr. L. said it was okay. Catie scarfed down three bowls of it. And guess what? She didn't throw up.

The following day Larry left to get back to the boys. Catie was up and about. Her chest tube had been removed and she only had a few more days in the hospital. She gave Larry big hugs and kisses. "Bye Daddy. I love you."

After he left, Catie turned to me and said, "You know, Mom,

I don't mind having surgery. Wanna know why? Because I know that Daddy will be here when I come out."

I just looked down at her in amazement. She could see the bright side of anything. And I thought, *Catie, could you teach me to be more like you?*

Chapter 13

We Are Family

Coming from a large, loving family meant that we were always involved in each other's lives. I have five brothers and sisters. It also meant that Catie's diagnosis devastated each and every one of my siblings and broke my parents' hearts. But Catie was the one to show us the way through this journey. Her lighthearted joy and unending optimism meant that we could not let this disease take over our lives. We had to live our lives and live them with joy if we were to follow Catie's lead.

When my sister Anne Marie came to New York to visit us, she was apprehensive about seeing Catie sick. But her fears were allayed when, as she stepped out of the taxi, Catie came running out of the Ronald McDonald House in her pajamas and slippers to meet her. "Aunt Re, Aunt Re. You made it! I can't believe you're here. Come on in. I want to show you our room. And then we will go to the hospital. And then later we are going to go to Benihana's!"

Catie managed to tire out both me and Anne Marie during her visit. We went to the Museum of Natural History, Central Park, Benihana's and any other place Catie could talk us into. Anne Marie has a whole series of photos she took of Catie in the park, getting her nails done, and just being Catie. She taught her Aunt the shortcut to the hospital, how to hail a cab, and how to have fun.

Going to the hospital was tough for my sister. We were living in that cancer world, but Anne Marie was getting her first exposure to it. I remember her face as she walked into the clinic. Shell-shocked. Probably how I looked the first time I saw it.

"Gina, I was so scared to see all of those sick kids. It just breaks my heart. But now I see that you guys are friends and you support each other. It is actually an amazing thing to watch." she told me. I introduced her to everyone – kids, parents, doctors, nurses. She began to understand that this crazy world in which we lived brought us comfort and friendship and even happiness.

When my brother Tony came out to visit, he said, "Gina, I was petrified to walk into Sloan-Kettering. I didn't know what to expect."

Well, what he saw was Catie sitting up in her hospital bed, chatting on the phone. The minute she saw Tony she said "I've got to go. Uncle Tuna is here." He started laughing and that was that. Tony's visit brightened both of our days. But I think that Catie brought some sunshine to him.

My younger sister Terry was devastated when she learned that Catie's cancer had come back. But she stood by me all the time, whatever we needed. Her visits to New York brought comfort to me and to Catie. And when Terry brought her daughter Tess with her, it was cause for celebration.

When we saw Sam and his family and Johnny and his family, I could tell that the sight of Catie – thin, bald and pale, was killing them. But she managed to work her magic on them. With her smiling face and her energy, she made all of us forget, for a time, that she had cancer.

My parents, Catie's Dommie and Papa, loved her so much. Whenever they would visit, Catie was beyond excited. My parents went down to Florida every year in the fall and would return in the spring. But Christmas was spent at our home in Ballston Lake. Catie would decorate their stockings and draw pictures for them. One cold December night, I was going to the Albany Airport to pick them up and Catie wanted to go with me. But she didn't want to get out of her pajamas. "Mom, I really want to go to the airport, but I don't want to get dressed. Pleaseeeeee let me go in my pajamas!" So there we were, Catie with her fuzzy pj's, winter coat and boots waiting for their plane to land. The minute she spotted them, she took off and launched herself into their arms. Having Dommie and Papa for Christmas was the best gift ever.

Catie's illness was hardest on her brothers Johnny and Robby. Johnny was only two when Catie was diagnosed. The first time he saw Catie after she had been in treatment he didn't believe that it was her. She looked skinny and had no hair. He kept saying, "That's not Catie! That's not Catie!"

But Catie just looked at him and smiled and said, "No Johnny, it's me. Catie. I just don't have any hair. I have to go to the hospital to get better and when I'm better I'll get my hair back. But it's me, Johnny. It's Catie."

After that, Johnny would say, "Catie has to go to the hossipal to get her hair back!"

Whenever we made it home, Robby wanted to sleep in the other twin bed in Catie's room. They played and laughed and talked. When he came to visit us at Sloan-Kettering, they sat in her hospital bed watching television and talking. One of the nurses walked in and said "Oh my God. Is that Catie's twin?"

We learned that you can be a family even when you are 150 miles away. That being together is the best gift. That making the most of our time together was the most important thing. That love spans any distance. Catie taught us that. Yes, we are family and those bonds are unbreakable.

Chapter 14

Happy Birthday To Me

Life goes on. Even when your child is in treatment for cancer. We learned that lesson really quickly. Celebrations could happen anytime, anywhere. Catie made sure of that.

She had just completed a really tough round of chemo. We knew the drill. Her counts were dropping and soon she would develop a fever. Then she would be hospitalized until they figured out which infection she had and how to treat it. Once her counts started to rise and her fever abated, we would be free.

The thing about this hospitalization was that it was taking place in January. On January 20, to be precise, my 40th birthday. I am not too superstitious, and many months earlier, long before Catie relapsed, I was in a party store. Invitations, napkins and plates for a 40th birthday were on sale. With some, but not too much, trepidation, I purchased them. I should have known better.

So here we were – in-patient at Sloan-Kettering. I knew how

important this day was to Catie. She loved parties and she loved giving gifts. She was determined to make this day special for me. She and the child-life specialist, Trish, had been plotting and planning for several days.

"Happy birthday, Mom. How does it feel to be 40? Do you feel old?" Catie asked.

As a matter of fact, I felt pretty ancient. Having a critically ill child will do that to you. On the other hand, that child was Catie and I would not want to be anywhere but with her. "No, Cate. I don't feel too old."

The previous day when we were still at the Ronald McDonald House, Catie announced to the whole dining room that now that I was turning 40 my eyesight was failing. "Yeah, since my mom is turning 40 everything is falling apart. She just had to get glasses. She can't see anything."

My friends all started laughing as Catie continued to enumerate my many age-related problems. All I could do was thank God that she didn't know how much I weighed or that too would have been broadcast to the group at large.

There we were, hanging out in her hospital room. I could see that she was bubbling over about something, but I didn't know what. When there was a knock at the door, Catie's face lit up. "Come in," she hollered.

There was Trish with a huge bouquet of flowers and a small gift-wrapped box. Trish slid them over to Catie so that she could present them to me. The tulips, my absolute favorite, were gorgeous, all shiny and pink. As I opened the small box, Catie's face brightened even more. Inside the jewelry box was a silver ladybug necklace. "Mom, I picked it out and paid for it myself when we were at Aunt Michelle's and Uncle Stephen's."

A few weeks earlier we had a visit with our very good friends who live in Westchester. Larry brought the boys down to their house and Steph picked up me and Catie so we could spend a family weekend at their home. I knew that Catie and Larry had been out for a while during the visit, but I didn't know what they were doing.

I had gone to law school in Buffalo with Michelle. Steph was a dental student living with law students. We all hung out together and had stayed friends since then. Michelle and Larry had worked together at the IRS in Manhattan. That set up led to our marriage and our three children. Our lives were intertwined. Michelle and Steph had Dylan three months before we had Catie. Our children were growing up knowing they had cousins in Westchester. It didn't matter that we weren't blood relatives. They were our family.

When I called them the day we learned Catie had cancer, Michelle's tears and her horrified "no" stated in no uncertain terms that this child of ours was part of their family. Since Catie's treatment brought us to New York City, their house had become our home away from home. They welcomed us any and every time we needed them.

It was on our previous visit that Catie had gone shopping. Larry and Steph had taken the kids with them on their outing while Michelle and I got to catch up. When they all arrived back at the house, I knew that something was up. That was when Catie had purchased my present.

"Catie, I love, love, love it. You have such beautiful taste in gifts. I will always wear this. Thank you, honey."

As I was admiring the flowers and necklace, we heard another knock on the door. There in the doorway were Lynn and Catie's friend Kevin. Lynn had wheeled him over in their stroller. They came to celebrate with us. A bottle of Champagne was tucked, or should I say hidden, in Kevin's seat. There was a really delicious scent coming from a bakery box.

"Happy birthday," cried Lynn and Kevin.

"Let's get this cork popped," said Lynn. I was not going to argue with her. The party had begun. The chocolate cake came out of the box. Candles were lit. Catie helped me blow them out because in my old age blowing out candles was getting difficult. Lynn and Kevin brought me scented candles to make our room at the Ronald McDonald House a little homier.

We checked on a few of the kids in the other rooms. "Shirley, come on over and have a glass of Champagne. You can bring Simon with you. We have cake!"

"Cheryl, can you get away for a few minutes while Jake is sleeping? There is Champagne waiting for you."

Catie was absolutely delighted to be able to present me with a party even though she was in the hospital. She definitely loved giving presents more than getting them.

As the nurses came in to check on Catie, they dug into the cake and I got happy birthday wishes from the whole pediatric floor. Who knew that turning 40 in a cancer center in New York City with a sick child could be so wonderful?

As I closed my eyes and blew out the candles on my cake, I made my wish. I wished that someday Catie would be using those napkins, plates and invitations for *her* 40th birthday.

Chapter 15

Angels On Earth

It is often said that doctors are not gods, that they are just humans. But I believe Catie's doctors were angels on earth. I learned so much from them. I think they also learned a little bit from Catie.

The fact that Catie needed to go to Memorial Sloan-Kettering Cancer Center in New York City was terrifying. When we first arrived, it felt like we had entered a MASH unit. I watched in disbelief as parents casually wandered around, chatting. Bald children were getting chemo and playing games. I thought there was no way I would ever be able to adapt to this setting. All I could foresee were crying jags and frequent trips to the ladies room.

It is amazing how quickly that changed. Sloan-Kettering had a team of neuroblastoma doctors. As we met each member of the team, we came to know, love and trust them. We were in awe as we watched them deal with sad or upset or frustrated parents. We came to admire them, not only for their excellent medical skills but also for their compassion. Our daughter's life was in their hands and they made us feel safe.

Larry had contacted Dr. Cheung as soon as we learned that Catie's cancer had returned. He was the chief doctor of the hospital's neuroblastoma team. When Larry called, he got through to Dr. Cheung immediately. He told us to bring Catie down the next day for an appointment. When we saw him, he reviewed all of Catie's medical records and ordered a slew of tests. Her first scan was scheduled for a Saturday morning in nuclear medicine. We were shocked and grateful to see him come in that morning to check on Catie and review the results. Often we would get an email from him at 11:30 p.m. or later, saying that he had reviewed her test results and had some ideas on how to best treat her.

Once, during a particularly tough week, I was losing it. Fear had taken over. Usually we parents tried to stay in control, at least in front of the kids. As he passed me in the busy waiting room, he asked how I was doing. I burst out crying and grabbed his hand. "Dr. Cheung, please save my daughter."

He took me by the arm and led me to a small conference room. Catie was playing in the playroom. He handed me a box of tissues and let me cry. He sat and talked to me until I had calmed down and could face the cancer world again. This man, who is so dedicated to his work that he rented an apartment in the city to be closer to the hospital, did not make me feel like I was an imposition. He gave me as much time as I needed.

Another time, as I passed him in the hallway, I casually mentioned that Catie had a headache. "Okay," he said. "We're going to set her up with a CT scan right now." I was so grateful that he took everything seriously. That he listened to us. That he made sure Catie got the best treatment she could.

One day a bunch of us moms wrote "What Doctors Say, What Parents Hear" and shared it with the doctors. One of the things we discussed was the anxiety around scan time. We wrote: "It is very hard to wait for test results. Please don't get angry when we keep asking to see the reports. To you it may just be a test. But to us, it is our child's life. Please be patient with our tears and our fears."

About a week later Dr. Cheung came up to me on a Friday morning. "We have the results of Catie's latest scans. How about we go over them on Mon…" and then caught himself. "Let's meet today after lunch to go over them." I think I loved him a little bit more that day.

When we first got to the hospital and a treatment plan was established, we met with Dr. Kushner who went over the protocol. He met with all three of us and explained everything to Catie. She listened to everything that was going to happen to her – the chemo, the surgeries, the radiation, the scans. And she just nodded her head and said, "Okay. I can do that."

Dr. Kushner looked at her with admiration and said, "That sounds good, Catie."

When Catie and Kevin would "borrow" medical supplies and build their forts, he would just shake his head and laugh. He never was too busy to have some fun with the kids. When the kids wrote their book, "Doctor Destroyer," he was one of the doctors who made it out alive.

Dr. Kramer, the third neuroblastoma doctor, became our very special friend. Kim would laugh as Catie buzzed around the clinic giving her a status report on each kid. When Catie was in-patient, she would come in Catie's room during rounds and end up sitting there and chatting with us for quite a while.

One day Catie wanted to Rollerblade to the hospital.

"Mom, I know I can do it! Please let me Rollerblade. It's not that far."

"Okay, honey. But you are wearing a helmet, knee pads and wrist pads. And you can't go too fast. I don't want to have to run to keep up with you, Miss Tish."

So Catie Rollerbladed to the hospital, took the elevator to the clinic floor and proceeded to Rollerblade down all the halls and past all of the examination rooms. Dr. Kramer looked at her in amazement.

"Well, I guess I don't have to do a neurological exam. Her balance and reflexes are great and she obviously has energy," she laughed.

I knew how much Catie meant to her on the day we were waiting for some very important test results. I watched Dr. Kramer pick up the phone in the hallway to call the radiologist. As I watched her face react to the news, she put her forehead against the phone and banged her hand in frustration against the cinderblock wall. When she turned away from me and went directly into the office I knew the news was bad. I knew that she didn't want to be the one to tell me. You become very good at reading the signs on the faces of the doctors.

Dr. Laquaglia was Catie's surgeon. When other doctors at other hospitals would say it was crazy to operate on certain tumors, Dr. Laquaglia would go in and get the whole thing. He operated on Catie several times, performing three thoracotomies and removing three-fourths of her liver. All of us parents were grateful every day that he was "crazy" enough to operate on our kids.

At one critical point in Catie's treatment, Larry and I met with the whole team. Each armed with our own legal pad, we proceeded to ask pages of questions. Dr. Cheung asked, "Are you guys engineers?"

"Nope, lawyers."

The whole team cracked up. "Now it makes sense."

But they made sure that each and every one of our questions was answered.

One day Dr. LaQuaglia was showing me and Catie one of her scans. Catie looked at it and turned to him and said "Dr. Laquaglia, this scan is backwards."

He looked at it, looked at Catie, looked at the scan again and said, "You are absolutely right." Then he burst out laughing.

"Catie, some day you are going to be running this hospital," he said.

I looked at him with hope in my eyes. "Sounds great to me."

These doctors meant the world to us parents. Our hopes rested in their hands. And we knew that they were doing everything that they could to save our children. Angels on earth? Absolutely.

Chapter 16

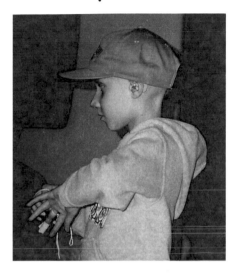

Listen Up

It always amazed me what we parents were willing to do to try to save our children. What amazed me even more was how Catie could handle the not so good and turn it into something special.

The chemotherapy on the N7 protocol basically brought the kids near death. The chemo meant that their counts were zero – minuscule red, white and platelet cells. The hope was that the chemo would take care of any renegade cancer cells still floating through their bodies.

The N7 called for seven rounds of chemo. Weeks one, three, five and seven were tough. Catie was nauseous and exhausted. In the morning, she would climb into the jogging stroller. "Catie, do you have the tissues and vomit basin?" I would ask as we trudged out of the Ronald McDonald House. We would make our way to Sloan-Kettering for another day of cancer treatment.

Weeks two, four and six were even worse. Catie couldn't eat a thing for a week. The vomiting was pretty constant. The doctors were concerned when the kids started losing weight. Catie was weighed every day. Each time she hovered just above the tipping point. If she dipped below that point, the doctors planned to insert a feeding tube. We did not want that! So every time her weight was even a fraction of a pound over the magic number, we did a happy dance.

One of the side effects of the chemo, in addition to the vomiting, fatigue and hair loss, was hearing loss. Throughout the treatment, I felt like parts of Catie were being taken from us with each round. Her vibrant, happy, healthy self was being turned into a sickly child. No color in her cheeks, no hair on her head, no meat on her bones. Partway through the protocol, Catie had her hearing tested. After the test, which took over two hours, the doctor turned to me and said, "Her hearing is perfect!"

Yay, I thought, *maybe Catie will be one of the miracle kids who doesn't lose her hearing. Maybe this one side effect would skip her!*

Once she completed the protocol, it was back for another test. This time the hearing loss was quite apparent. The doctor explained the results to me, but I don't think I could comprehend them at the time. As I wheeled her back to the clinic I could feel the tears running down my face. I didn't want Catie to know how upset I was. It seemed so unfair. These kids were going through torture in the hopes that they might live. But they were giving up so much. They were missing school, missing their friends, missing playdates and sleepovers. To lose their hearing on top of everything seemed particularly cruel.

Catie viewed this as just one more obstacle to be overcome. When we went home we had an appointment with a hearing specialist. She figured out what Catie needed and we were set to order the hearing aids. While we were looking at the clear and beige ones, Catie announced, "I would like the multicolor glitter ones!"

So Catie got her glitter hearing aids. She managed to make it to school for a day when we were home during the week. She loved going into her classroom, seeing her teacher, playing with her friends. I wasn't sure if she was going to get teased for having hearing aids. I should have known better. The kids in her class were so happy to see her and they thought the hearing aids were cool.

A few weeks later, the mom of one of Catie's friends called me and said, "Listen to this. Jeannette stayed home with an earache today, but I'm not sure it really was an earache."

"Why not?" I asked.

Because she said, "Mom, my ears really hurt. I think I need hearing aids. Can I get glitter ones like Catie's?"

Leave it to Catie to make hearing aids a fashion accessory!

Chapter 17

Prom

Prom. The word conjures up dresses and tuxedos and flowers and food. Does it conjure up bald little heads and chemotherapy and surgery? At Sloan-Kettering it did. But for one magical day, those were set aside. Prom was a day for fun, for memories, for leaving the cancer world for a little while.

Having fun was our main priority in New York (after, of course, trying to find a cure for this disease.) We knew that if Catie had something to look forward to, the treatments would be easier to tolerate. She would say "Mom, do you think we can go to Benihana's tonight when I'm done with chemo? Kevin and Lynn could come too."

"Sure" I would say. "Let me talk to Lynn and see what their schedule is like." Lynn and Kevin thought it was a great idea. So once the kids were done, we headed back to the Ronald McDonald House and dropped off our hospital stuff.

Catie and Kevin would rush to the corner of 73rd Street and 1st Avenue, their hands in the air, waving for a cab. I think hailing a cab is one of the first things Catie learned in New York. We would take the cab to the Japanese steakhouse, first stopping off to get a bottle of Kraft barbecue sauce for Catie. The chefs would show off even more for the kids, their chopping becoming more extravagant, the food flying higher and faster. We all loved it. And we moms got to order a beer with dinner. Yeah!!

Another favorite was Jekyll and Hyde, a kind of macabre restaurant with Frankensteins and ghosts and talking animal heads. We went there so often that the wolf head on the wall, Toby, would say "I smell Catie tonight" which of course would send Catie into hysterics. One night she and Kevin were invited onto the stage to sing and dance to the theme song. It involved a lot of clapping and finger snapping, and of course, laughter. If the kids weren't bald, no one would have known they were sick.

It wasn't all fun and games. If Kevin wasn't feeling well, Catie would hover by his bedside. "Do you think he needs benadryl, or maybe an ativan?" Catie would ask as the doctors or nurses came to check on him. And the doctors or nurses would look at his chart and decide if maybe Catie had "prescribed" the right medicine.

During one round of treatment, Catie had to go back to the Ronald McDonald House with a backpack full of chemo. It was a 24 hour infusion so it had to be running through the night. Kevin, watching her struggle with the pack said "Catie, let me carry the chemo backpack." and he slung it over his shoulder as they walked to the arcade room. I caught Lynn's eye and she smiled at me as we both thought how very lucky we were to all have found each other.

As the month of May was approaching the talk in the hospital was all about the prom. Sloan-Kettering really knows how to throw a party. The excitement was palpable. Kids and parents were discussing "What color dress are you going to wear?" "Are they providing tuxes for the boys?" "Do you think we will get flowers?"

As Catie and I pored over pictures of dresses, she said "I don't want to wear a frilly one. I really want to wear my pink Tweety Bird dress with my flip flops." And so of course that is what she wore.

We all had fun decorating what was to be the prom carriage. Before it was decorated, it kind of looked like a big glass crib. We made Kleenex flowers and had crepe paper strung from one end of the "carriage" to the other. The playroom was transformed. Tablecloths, flowers, platters of food, a dance floor. Before the event the girls were offered tiaras and headbands. They didn't need bows and barrettes because they didn't have hair. The boys were given boutonnières and the girls' corsages. The kids were transported into the playroom in the carriage. The DJ and his helpers were energetic, getting everyone on the floor dancing.

Catie and Kevin were twirling around to the music. The only problem was that Kevin was still attached to his IV line, getting an antibiotic. So as the kids boogied, Lynn raced around after them, untangling Kevin's line after each spin. My daughter was wearing sunglasses, silver beads with a neon peace sign and singing into the microphone, with her hands waving above her head.

And then there were the moms. As we snacked on mini quiches and pigs in the blanket and watched the kids, it was impossible not to have fun. As we lined up in a row, Aretha Franklin was playing and we all started dancing and singing "R-E-S-P-E-C-T, Find out what it means to me." The doctors and nurses joined us and by the end of the afternoon. We were all sweaty, happy and tired.

We parents all knew enough to make the most of this day. As we laughed and chatted and smiled at the kids, our hearts were obviously hoping that one day we would see them off to their high school proms. But for now, this moment in time, the Sloan-Kettering prom was more than enough. It was a gift.

Chapter 18

Tessie

There was nothing like visitors from home to brighten our days. When my sister made plans to bring her daughter down for a visit, Catie and I were absolutely thrilled. For days we made plans. FAO Schwarz, Benihana's, Central Park. We were going to fit in as much as possible.

"Tessie!" cried Catie with a big smile as she pranced barefoot toward the sidewalk. She had her IV bag slung over her shoulder, but it didn't slow her down. She had spotted the taxi carrying my five-year-old niece and my sister Terry, and she wanted to make sure that she was right by their door as they exited. As Catie ran down the steps of Sloan-Kettering, I caught my sister's eye and we grinned at each other. We were having a girls' weekend in New York. Catie didn't care that she had just had a very long week of chemotherapy. She just wanted to have fun with her cousin. Since Catie didn't have to go back to the hospital for anything that weekend, we were set to enjoy ourselves.

After convincing Catie that she needed shoes on her feet, we climbed into another taxi and headed to one of Catie's favorite restaurants, Benihana's. She wanted to show Tess the Japanese chefs who chopped food with flair, flung it into their chef's hats and tossed it into the mouths of the people sitting at the table. Of course, we had to bring Kraft's barbecue sauce and we had to order the soup with no vegetables. The kids were beyond excited. It was so good to see two little cousins just enjoying being together. I was thrilled to have my little sister with me.

After dinner we headed back to the Ronald McDonald House where Catie gave them the tour. Both kids loved the idea of being able to go down to the game room. They could play all of the arcade games for free and sodas were only a quarter. Terry and I hung out and played ping-pong with them. Catie was very proud to show Tess all of the toys and crafts and games. About 9 p.m. we were finally ready to go back to our room.

The next morning we were off to Central Park. One of the volunteers at the Ronald McDonald House who learned that we were going to spend the day at the park offered us tickets to the Central Park Zoo. We headed to her apartment and she got to meet the kids while we chatted for a few minutes. Then it was off to the zoo.

Central Park had so much to offer and we wanted to do everything. All four of us were clamoring "I want to see the sea lions," and "I want cotton candy," After we walked around a bit, we headed to the horse and carriage rides. We had never taken a tour around the park and the kids really wanted to. Yes, it is touristy, but it is also great fun. As we were seated in a carriage being pulled by a horse around the middle of Manhattan, it felt like a dream. We were surrounded by people, hot dog vendors and cars honking their horns in the midday traffic. Huge buildings and gorgeous old hotels encircle the park. We had a great vantage point, being able to see the beauty of Central Park and the craziness of a New York City street.

From there we went to FAO Schwarz. This is the mecca of all toy stores, a three-story toy heaven with dolls, giant keyboards, electronic toys and every other thing a child could want. Toy soldier guards opened the doors for us. Tess was absolutely mesmerized. Her eyes popped when she saw the hundreds of stuffed animals. She was awed by the sheer quantity of toys in front of her. Catie had been there many, many times, so she was all set to show Tess the ropes. We told the kids they could each pick out one thing, anything they wanted. Catie decided on a small set of musical instruments. Tess chose a flower that opened up with little people and a swing. The kids clung to those toys as we continued on our trek through New York.

Next we went to the Warner Bros. store. When the girls decided they needed new clothing, we let them each pick out an outfit. Tess chose a Scooby Doo skort and cute little top. Catie, a huge Tweety fan, selected navy Tweety shorts trimmed in lime green with a matching shirt.

We had dinner at Jekyll and Hyde, the macabre restaurant that Catie absolutely loved. As we entered through the spooky elevator with spider webs hanging in our faces and skeletons in the back, Catie told Tess, "We have to go see Toby the wolf. He's really nice." Tess didn't look convinced. Maybe the mummies and the skeletons had something to do with that. The hostess showed us to our table and immediately the kids went off to see Toby.

At first we all thought it was some kind of mechanized voice, until we heard, "Is that Catie I smell?" Both kids squealed with delight. Even Terry and I jumped.

When we made it back home to the Ronald McDonald House, we were all very, very happy. I'm not sure if the kids were tired, but Terry and I were exhausted. Since our twin beds were pushed together, Tess and Catie shared one half, I occupied the other half. Terry got the rollaway cot. Terry, Catie and I had a good laugh once Tess fell asleep because Tess snored like no one we had ever heard. Buzz saw, train locomotive, you name it and this kid snored louder. I kept looking at this little peanut of a girl, saying, "Where is that noise coming from?"

The next day was Sunday and the Ronald McDonald House was having a party on the roof. Tess and Terry thought this was the coolest thing ever.

"How will we get up there? How will we get down?" Tess asked.

But Catie, who thought of herself as world-wise, told Tess, "Don't worry. I'll show you how to do it." Catie was definitely a New Yorker now.

The day was sunny and beautiful. Were on the roof with a bunch of other kids and their families. A woman dressed as the Statue of Liberty was handing out candy. This was a celebration with face painting and balloon animals and lots of hot dogs and hamburgers. The kids got glow-in-the-dark necklaces and patriotic hats. Tess and Catie had their new Scooby Doo and Tweety outfits on and they joined in with the kids surrounding the Statue of Liberty.

I introduced Terry to some of my friends. She put faces to the names I mentioned over the year. "So this is Spencer! So nice to finally meet you. And your mom Kathy," Terry said. "Is this little guy Jacob? He is adorable." She met Brianna and Allie and John and Simon, some of the kids fighting neuroblastoma like Catie.

As Tess and Catie were running around on the roof, Terry and I looked at our watches. We knew the time was approaching when she and Tess would have to get a cab back to Penn Station to take the train to Albany. Without a word being spoken, we told each other how very wonderful it was to spend a weekend with just us girls. For a whole weekend we were just two sisters and two cousins taking on Manhattan.

Chapter 19

Hot Stuff

Treatment for neuroblastoma is not easy. At Sloan-Kettering, that meant surgeries, and at least seven rounds of chemotherapy. It also meant a stem cell transplant with Catie's own cells. As one doctor described it, they basically bring the children close to death in order to save them.

Catie's treatment involved harvesting her stem cells, giving her radioactive antibodies and then giving her the stem cells back to recover from the radiation. The plan was for us to stay in her hospital room for a week. She had to be in isolation because she would be radioactive. Everyone dreaded the "hots." It meant being away from the other kids and not being able to go to the playroom. The nurses couldn't spend more than a minute in the room because of the radiation.

Harvesting the stem cells sounds worse than it was. When Catie started treatment, she had a broviac put in her chest. Two tubes protruded out of it. This allowed the doctors and nurses to administer drugs or draw blood without her having to be stuck by needles. It was no big deal when they hooked her up to the harvesting machine and in one day harvested enough cells for the treatment. She was lucky it went so smoothly. Many children had bone marrow involvement and harvesting of their stem cells was not easy.

Catie and I prepared for the "hots" by gathering as many craft supplies as we could and by decorating the room. "Mom, if we have to be here for a week I want the room to look fun." We got to work drawing pictures and decorating the walls. Her window was one big happy meadow scene, filled with trees and ladybugs and animals. The walls were covered in flowers. The nurses liked our room so much they had us leave everything up for the next kid.

Larry came down the first weekend. We thought it was going to be a tough week and Catie wanted her Daddy. He brought Catie a bunch of balsam airplanes. We would hear the nurses say, "Where are all these airplanes coming from?" as they watched the planes flying through the hallways. We thought that the hysterical laughter coming from Catie's room would have been a clue.

"Dad, do you think we'll get in trouble for doing this?" she said as she sent yet another airplane down the corridor. She was hiding behind her door, just one arm peeking out poised to send another plane flying.

"Well, Cate, as your attorney I don't think they have much proof against you. I think you're safe. But don't worry, I will represent you if you get arrested."

We settled in and got ourselves comfortable. It was a large room with two beds and a private bathroom. I got to sleep in a bed, not a fold-up chair. Yeah!

Each day a lead-lined cart was wheeled in. The doctor came and removed the radioactive antibodies from it. A syringe was used to inject them into Catie's central line. Usually within a few minutes, the pain would start.

"Mom, it's starting. It really hurts."

"Kateri, Catie's in pain. We need oxymorphone," I would announce into the intercom. A few minutes later our nurse would hurry in and quickly give Catie the narcotic. She couldn't stay in the room because of the radiation. After a few hours, Catie, having been knocked out by the drugs, would wake up. Then the fun would begin again.

Catie and I decided to hold an ice cream tasting contest. Which butter pecan was truly the best? Ben & Jerry's or Haagen Dazs? We threw in a few chocolate flavors for variety. Every day we would "sample" the ice cream. Sample meaning huge scoops that barely fit in the bowl. At the end of the week we decided Ben & Jerry's deserved the prize. We wanted to share our ice cream with the nurses. Our only problem was the ice cream scoop. We had to make sure that it stayed in the room because it too became radioactive. And because it was radioactive we couldn't use it to scoop ice cream for them. Oh, well, more for us.

Catie developed an addiction to Benadryl. She liked the way it put her to sleep. Every night we would watch the "Brady Bunch." If she wasn't sleepy by the end of the show, she would ring the call button to ask for it. I tried to give it a little time to see if she could get to sleep without it. But I swear she made herself stay awake late enough so that she could get a dose. I was slumped over in my chair, exhausted, and she would be chattering away until she got it.

"Catie, when you are done with this cancer treatment, I think we are going to have to put you in rehab for your addiction to Benadryl." She would just laugh.

We knew we had a long several days in front of us and we wanted to make sure we had plenty to do. "Mom, let's make some puppets and have a puppet show." I could come and go, so I ran to the playroom to get supplies. I brought felt, scissors, glitter and glue. Each day we made a bunch of animal puppets. Catie had a great time writing the script. We practiced every day.

There was a lead shield in the middle of the room. I was

supposed to stay on one side, Catie on the other. Well, that was a laugh because what mom is going to let a lead shield come between her and her child in pain? On Catie's last day of treatment, we invited the nurses to see the show. They hovered in the doorway, smiling as Catie put on her play. The child-life specialist even videotaped it for us.

And we did find a use for that lead shield. It made a perfect stage for a puppet show.

Chapter 20

A Ministry Of Magic

Whenever we made it back home, we would try to have a party so Catie could see friends and family. One special weekend, she made her First Holy Communion. Corpus Christi worked with us on making this day special. Everyone in the parish saw her shining face and big smile as she received the host.

As I looked at her in little white communion dress, my tears flowed. The whole family was there. I saw the broken-hearted looks on their faces. We knew we probably were not going to see her walk down the aisle and get married. Catie kept looking at me and asking, "Why are you crying, Mom?"

I wiped my eyes and smiled, saying, "Because I am so happy and proud of you, honey."

Through our tears, we were determined to have a great time. We were only home for the weekend from Sloan-Kettering and we were thrilled that family from all over could make it to the event. Catie was so excited about the party after church.

"Mom, look I got the first two Harry Potter books!" Catie exclaimed. As she continued to open her gifts, I asked, "Who is Harry Potter?"

My sister-in-law Laurie looked at me in disbelief. "You don't know who Harry Potter is? He is only the biggest sensation since the Beatles!" She had given Catie the books.

The next day Catie and I took the train back to New York City. She decided that I should read the books to her. From the first page, we were hooked. Harry's wizardry and magic were enthralling for all children, especially to kids with cancer going through treatment. His adventures and his courage brought joy and magic to us all.

I read to her non-stop; when she was having chemotherapy, when she was recovering from surgery, during her many scans. At night, every night, I read to her. Once when she was having radiation, I wasn't allowed in the room. So the technicians set it up so I could read to her over the intercom. The big surprise was for the other patients receiving radiation. "What's going on?" they asked. "Who is this Harry Potter? Why are we hearing about him over the PA system?" Everyone got a dose of Harry that day, whether they needed it or not. Not one person complained. We purchased the books on tape and Catie listened to them on her own.

When we made it home again over Thanksgiving, a local library was having a Harry Potter party. I called to see if they could fit Catie in, but they were already full. When I happened to mention it to a friend, she said, "Hold on a minute." After a quick phone call, she came back and said, "Catie's in. They have room for her."

The party was scheduled for a Sunday afternoon. We had to take Amtrak back to New York City later that day to be ready for treatment on Monday. Catie was beyond excited about the party. When she got home, she had on a cape, Harry Potter glasses and was sporting a zigzag scar on her forehead, just like Harry. She didn't want to get changed. Catie wasn't one to be shy about looking a little different. She ruled the aisles of the train that day looking like Harry. The joy in her face brought smiles to the other passengers.

In the midst of our reading frenzy, Catie asked, "Mom, can we write to J.K. Rowling? Maybe she will send us a picture of Harry!"

"OK, Cate. Let's see what we can find." We searched the Internet, looking for any type of email address. We weren't successful. She wanted the author to know how much Harry Potter meant to her, how much his antics amused her and kept her mind off her battle with cancer. We just couldn't figure out how to reach her.

Until one day, a very special day, as Catie and I sat at the computer, a new email popped up. The sender's name was Joanne Rowling. "What?" we screamed in unison. "How did this happen?"

"Dear Catie," it read, "Your friend Paul Steinberg has written to me to tell me how much you like the Harry Potter books and I can't tell you how much it meant to me. I am working very hard on book four at the moment – on a bit that involves some new creatures Hagrid has brought along for the Care of Magical Creatures classes. This is all TOP SECRET, so you are allowed to tell Paul, Simon and your mom and nobody else, or you'll be getting an owl from the Ministry of Magic for giving our secrets away to Muggles. With lots of love, J.K. Rowling (Jo to anybody in Gryffindor)."

And so it began. The emails between Scotland and New York flew back and forth faster than any owl could fly. Every time Jo's name popped up in our inbox, Catie and I would both start screaming.

"Mom," Catie said, "I really want to send Jo a gift." She decided on chocolate frogs and a magic wand, both very important in the Harry Potter books.

Jo sent Catie a cat and an owl that looked just like Pigwidgeon. Jo said to Catie, "I'm so glad you liked your very late birthday presents. I had loads of fun buying them. The woman in the shop where I bought your cat thought I was a bit odd. I saw him on a shelf over her head and said 'Crookshanks!' very loudly. She definitely wasn't a Harry Potter reader … Lots of love, Jo x x x x x x x x x x x x x x x"

Catie and I didn't know how to pronounce the name of one of the characters, so we asked Jo. "OK, the correct pronunciation of Hermione is Her-my-oh-nee." We were definitely way off on that one.

Catie liked to tell Jo about her favorite places in New York. Jo responded, "What is Beni Hana's??? And what's at the Little Shop of Plaster??? You see, when I go to New York, I am usually being rushed around in cars to go and do book signings and things, so I don't get to see as much as I would like. You'll have to tell me some really good places to go next time I come."

Another note from Jo said, "Sorry I didn't answer yesterday – I was working away from home and I didn't have my Internet lead with me, so I couldn't check emails. I'm really glad you had such a lovely Valentine's Day. I got two cards – one from you, of course, and one Jessica made at school … Yes, just between ourselves, I am convinced your mom is a witch. Getting into Honeydukes would be a bit difficult from New York, though unless she's got a very fast broomstick or a hippogriff. She'll just have to find the Diagon Alley of New York – all major cities have one. I suspect that the entrance might be somewhere near West Broadway. There are a number of likely looking little sidestreets around there where you could find a mysterious bar, unseeable to the Muggle eye."

No matter what was happening during Catie's treatment, an email from Jo made everything better. Her kindness and willingness to take the time to write to Catie show that J.K. Rowling is much more than an author. She is a sorceress who brought joy and excitement to a very sick child. While there is no magical cure for cancer, Jo certainly brought magic to our lives.

Chapter 21

Take Me Out To The Ball Game

Growing up in Boston, Larry was an avid Patriots fan and he also loved the Red Sox, which caused a bit of a problem in the family because Catie loved the Yankees. We were never quite able to figure out her attraction to the sport or to the team. But she loved them. And Larry, loving his daughter as he did, switched his allegiance to the team that most Red Sox fans hated!

To say that Catie was a huge Yankee fan would be a major understatement. She had jackets, hats and T-shirts. On any given day, Catie would be hooked up to chemo or wandering the halls with her Yankee clothes on. She was never without her favorite pin from her nurse Joan, and she kept her word that she wouldn't tell anyone where it came from.

Being in treatment at Sloan-Kettering meant living in New York City. And living in New York City meant that going to a Yankee game was first on Catie's wish list. This was back when you could take a subway to the Bronx and walk up to the ticket booth for a seat. And the prices were cheap.

On a beautiful spring day, Lynn and I decided to take Catie and Kevin to an afternoon game. Catie needed to have her blood counts checked and Kevin needed to be examined by the doctor. So we headed to the hospital as early as possible.

The finger-stick lady knew that this was a special day. "Come on in, Catie, we're going to get you out of here quickly!" The technician who analyzed the blood had Catie sit next to her while her white and red cells were counted. Catie could barely sit still she was so excited. We were relieved that everything was fine. We were good to go! Now we just had to grab Kevin. Lynn managed to get him sprung pretty quickly. We were on our way.

We trudged toward the subway with Lynn lugging her big bag of medical supplies. That bag was filled with bandages, dressing changes, purell – anything a cancer kid might need.

When a patient is undergoing chemotherapy he or she really needs to be very careful about germs. And here we were, bringing the kids on the subway! There was a whole lot of "Don't touch that," "Don't sit there "and "Please, please don't tell the doctors we took the subway," but we finally got there. Poor Lynn got stuck struggling with that bag to get it down into the subway and then back up when we got to the Bronx. By this point she was now practically dragging it.

When we got off the train, there were three fire trucks sitting around. Catie and Kevin immediately ran over to them. When the firefighters saw the kids, they reached out to us. With excited grins on their faces, Catie and Kevin got to check out the truck and sit in the front, all the while entertaining these unbelievably friendly and sweet guys. A picture of the two grinning kids with all of these big muscular firefighters graced our walls for several years.

We got our tickets and went to our seats. Up and up and up we went. Lynn was still dragging along the bag and we almost couldn't fit it in our seats. We were in the nosebleed section, which if you have low platelets can be a problem. Platelets help blood clot and chemo can make your platelets low. So if you happen to get a nosebleed, it probably won't stop and you may end up in the hospital. But the kids were tough and we were raring to go. They were not even thinking about cancer and chemo and radiation and surgery. It was all about baseball and having fun.

One major problem was that we were so high up, we couldn't get to the cotton candy. We could smell the hot dogs and popcorn, but it was cotton candy we wanted. Whenever the cotton candy guy was in our field of vision, Catie would say, "Mom, get him to come up here!"

I kept telling Catie, "I can't look down!" And he wouldn't look up. Around the seventh inning we caught the eye of the vendor and he came up to us. We finally got our cotton candy. That sweet, sticky, sugary treat was perfect!

The game was fantastic. Catie was getting hoarse from yelling so much. When Tino Martinez hit a grand slam, I thought Catie was going to jump onto the field. I said, "Catie, a grand slam is really rare. I think Tino hit it for you!" I love that she believed me. At the end of the game, we trudged back to the subway – two very tired moms and two very happy kids.

What amazed me was how these two kids put cancer out of their minds. They focused on what was in front of them. A Yankee game! They didn't care that they had no hair, that they couldn't touch anything, that they got tired walking to and from the subway. If only we parents could do the same.

Several days later, as we were leaving the Ronald McDonald House, Catie was approached and asked if she wanted to ring the first bell of the New York Stock Exchange and then throw out the first pitch of the Mets game – on television!

Without missing a beat, my daughter said, "No thanks, I'm a Yankees fan!"

Chapter 22

Wishful Thinking

It is a bittersweet feeling when you learn that your child qualifies for a Make-A-Wish trip. On the one hand, I was delighted that Catie could pick anything she wanted. On the other hand, she qualified because she had a life-threatening illness. But we were thrilled knowing that for several days, we would be together as a family.

"Hey Catie, come and meet Sue and Janet. They're from Make-A-Wish."

"Hi Sue, hi Janet. I'm Catie. How are you?"

"We're great. We want to talk to you about your wish."

We had returned home from Sloan-Kettering the day before. We knew that Catie had relapsed, but we didn't know what the next treatment was going to be. A relapse at this point meant there was no real chance for a cure. So we wanted to try to get her wish in before the new chemo started. We only had about a two-week window – not a lot of time for our wish-granters.

"Well, I want to go to Disney. We've never been there and I really like rides – even scary ones."

"Okay, Catie. We'll get right on it."

And they did. A week later we were on a flight to Orlando. We were picked up in a limousine around 6:00 in the morning. Our friends were peering out their windows as the white limo drove away, honking its horn.

Our wish granters met us at the airport with donuts and gifts to take on our trip. After we were seated and waiting for the rest of the passengers, one of the flight attendants approached. "We hear we have a celebrity on the plane. Catie, the pilot would like to meet you."

So Catie headed up to the cockpit wearing her denim jacket and her trademark smile. When she returned, the smile was even bigger. She was wearing pilot wings on her jacket and a pilot cap on her head. We landed in Orlando and picked up our rental car. The day was gorgeous.

Because Make-A-Wish had such little time to plan the trip, we weren't going to be able to stay at "Give Kids the World," a village with great cottages and ice cream shops dedicated to sick children. Even though we didn't stay there overnight, we got to visit it.

Make-A-Wish put us up in the Intercontinental Hotel, which was great because the tram ran right through it. Catie was eight years old, Robby seven and Johnny just turned four. This meant that if any of us got tired, we could just head back to the room for a nap.

The minute we entered the Disney Park, we were treated like royalty. Catie was given a big pin that said she was a special guest. We didn't have to wait in one line. The kids were thrilled. They rode the roller coasters over and over, even when Larry and I pooped out. Catie kept going strong. Nothing was going to stop her. If one of the traveling photographers spotted us, they took our pictures and gave us free copies.

Of course, this was August and it was brutally hot. The park was selling these water bottles with fans attached for $10. Trying to be frugal, we said, "We don't need those – they're too expensive!" Hah. After an hour in the baking sun we couldn't hand over the money fast enough.

In the afternoons we would head back to the hotel for some rest and relaxation. It had a beautiful pool and the kids loved it there.

"Mom, can I get a bikini?" Catie asked. Catie now had two scars on her back from her lung surgeries and a big scar on her stomach from her liver surgery, which our doctor described as looking like the Mercedes Benz symbol.

"Sure, Catie. But are you okay with people seeing your scars?"

"Moooom, really? I know I have my scars. I don't care. I just want a bikini."

So she got one. Boy, did she look cute, scars and all. She and her brothers had a blast in the pool, running around, jumping in, swimming like fish. I could take a lesson from her.

It was such a special time – to be together as a family with nothing to do but have fun. Worry was always at the back of our minds, but Larry and I wanted this to be the best family trip ever. But sustained fun can be exhausting. Except for Catie. She was raring to go every minute of every day.

After four days at Disney, Johnny started to get tired. As a four-year-old in the brutally hot sun with so much stimulation, we knew he was going to hit the wall. We went to breakfast with some of the Disney characters. Goofy took Johnny's hat and then the fun began. Johnny chased Goofy around trying to kick him, while Larry chased Johnny around trying to stop him. Thank God Goofy is nice.

Later that same day, we were hanging out by the pool. Catie and Robby were jumping in and swimming around, laughing and splashing. We could tell that Johnny was getting cooked. Larry started to bring him back to the room to rest. Well, Johnny wanted no part of it. He started saying, "I hate Mommy, I hate Daddy, I hate Santa Claus and I hate Mickey Mouse!" We knew right then that he needed a nap. Just a typical day of a typical family vacation!

By the last day in Florida, we were all ready to get back home. We headed to the Rainforest Café for lunch where the kids were enchanted by the life-like animals. As we sat there, out of the corner of my eye I thought I saw something moving. I let out a yell because the elephant was lifting his trunk toward us. The kids laughed hysterically. By the end of the meal, Larry and I were almost face down in our food from exhaustion, but the kids were still going strong.

One of the nights there we let the kids hang out in one of the kid lounges where there are babysitters. It was right in the hotel and we were given a beeper if they needed to reach us. As Larry and I sat there enjoying a quiet dinner, I asked him, "What are we going to do if they can't save her?"

And Larry being Larry held my hand and said, "We will do everything we can and we will make the most of each day." And that is what we did.

Chapter 23

You Got To Have Friends

Catie showed us that friends can be apart for weeks or months at a time and it doesn't matter. Catie's friends showed us that even when you are young, you know that friendship matters, whether your friend is in school, sick at home or away at a hospital for cancer treatment.

One of our first weeks at the hospital, Catie's friend Ashley came down with her mom for a visit. I was so grateful that my friend Nancy brought Ashley to see Catie. It meant so much to all of us.

"Mom, I can't believe that Ashley's here. Where should we go? Can we take them to the toy store?" It was a joy watching Catie and Ashley have fun together, even for just a few hours. They didn't care that Catie wasn't feeling well, that she was tired. They were just happy to be together.

When Catie's friend Jeannette and her mom Lynne came to see her, Catie was ready to be the tour guide. "Mom, I'm going to show Jeannette the play room and then we are going to go on the roof. Later on you can find us in the basement playing foosball."

Lynne was a little nervous leaving Jeannette and Catie to roam the Ronald McDonald House without us, while we sat in one of the living rooms catching up. But Catie assured her that she knew the ropes and that it was just fine. She and Jeannette ran all over the place. And when we had to go to the hospital, Catie made sure that Jeannette met her friends and they all had a good time.

One weekend, when we finally made it home, Catie got invited to a sleepover. "Mom, Alex is having a sleepover birthday party. Please, can I go? Please? Please? Please?" Larry and I were torn. We wanted her home with us, but we knew that she really wanted to go to the party. When we finally decided to let her go, she was thrilled. The next day, the mom called me to tell me that Catie stayed up the latest of all the kids. She just did not want to miss a minute of the action.

Catie had joined a Brownie troop. She was not able to participate in many of the activities, but she did whatever she could. I stood there with tears in my eyes the day she crossed over the bridge to Girl Scouts with the other girls. Her face shone with joy and excitement. The other moms had tears in their eyes too and we shared smiles and hugs. As I watched my daughter, my sick, skinny, pale daughter, all I could see was the huge grin on her face. Another milestone we got to share.

Every trip home meant a party. Whether it was bowling or Jeepers or just McDonalds, the kids knew that when Catie was home, there was fun to be had. Watching Catie live in the present moment, not worrying about the future, was a lesson we learned over and over from her. The way her face would light up with excitement whenever she spotted a friend or cousin made us smile. And she made sure that we, too, lived in the moment. No moping around or sad faces. Life was to be enjoyed. Our daughter turned out to be an amazing teacher. What a gift to all of us.

Chapter 24

The First Day Of Third Grade

Many children dread going to school. The end of summer meant the end of fun. But not Catie. She really loved school. And she really wanted to be there for the first day of third grade. We didn't know how long she would be with us, but we knew that school was an important part of her life. We didn't want her to miss a minute of it.

"Mom, do you think I'll make it home for the first day of school?" Catie asked as we sat in the waiting area of the clinic at Sloan-Kettering. We had just learned she was going to have another thoracotomy, a surgery to remove as many tumors as possible from her lungs. It was the week before Labor Day. Catie was to start third grade on the following Tuesday.

"I don't know, honey. Let's ask Dr. LaQuaglia when we see him."

As we approached his office, Catie said, "Mom, I really want to start third grade with the rest of the kids."

"I know, honey. We'll do everything we can to get you there. I promise." But I was worried that it wasn't going to happen. She was scheduled to have surgery on a Friday. School started the following Tuesday.

"Hi Catie. How are you feeling? Are you ready for me to operate on you again?" asked Dr. LaQuaglia, a man we adored for many reasons, one of which is that he speaks *to* the children. They, in fact, are his patients. He is wonderful with the parents, but his way with the kids was beyond special. He didn't talk down to them and he listened to them.

"Dr. LaQuaglia, I know I need this surgery, but school starts next Tuesday and I really, really, really want to be there for the first day. What do you think?"

"Well, Cate, I think we need to get this surgery done and see if we can get you home. I'm not sure it's possible to get you there for the first day of school because you need time to heal, but if anyone can do it, you can."

"Thanks, and I'm pretty sure I will be going to school next Tuesday," she said. That girl knew what she wanted.

Catie had made it to school for only three days throughout the year of second grade. We had spent most of the year at Sloan-Kettering. The first time we made it home during a school week, Catie really wanted to go. I drove her in to school. She was so excited and I was so nervous. When I got home, I realized she had forgotten to wear her hat. All day long I paced around and wondered if she was being teased for having no hair.

When she got off the bus, I said, "Hi honey, how did it go?"

"Great," she said.

"Did anyone say anything about your hair," I asked.

"Yup," she replied.

When she said that, all I could think of is what little shit of a kid made fun of her. Some kid I'm sure I would like to drop kick across the playground.

When I asked her what the kids said, she looked at me and

smiled. "They said 'Hey Catie, it looks like your hair is growing in. It looks really cute.'"

I sent a silent thank you to those sweet children in second grade and thanked my lucky stars that I wouldn't have to beat up one of them.

The second time she was able to go to school, the kids were taking a math test. I asked her if she wanted to stay.

"Of course I want to stay," she replied.

Her teacher smiled at me and said, "How about if I drive her home at the end of the day?"

My thank you was laced with tears as I walked out of the classroom. She brought home a perfect score on her math test.

The third time she made it to school it was for the class play. Catie was so excited to be there and when the teacher asked her if she wanted to be in it, Catie jumped at the chance. She put on her bunny ears, the teacher drew whiskers on her face and for that whole day, Catie was just a regular second-grader. I know Catie's smile was bigger than mine and Larry's, but not by much.

So being there for the first day of third grade was really important. She wanted to start school like every other kid. We had our work cut out for us. Larry came down for the surgery. Catie was her usual trouper self. Once the anesthesia wore off, we got our charming Catie back. While it was wearing off was another story – she could be quite demanding. "I need a drink. I'm hungry. Why can't I walk around? Where is my doctor?" But we just laughed and waited for the other Catie to arrive.

Catie's surgery had gone well and Dr. LaQuaglia told us he would be in over the weekend to check on her.

After we got to see Catie in the recovery room, she was transferred to the pediatric observation unit (the Poo). She worked hard on the incentive spirometer to make sure her lungs were working. She had to suck hard on a tube to make a little ball rise up. This was especially important after a lung surgery. She still had a chest tube in, but she was doing pretty well.

"Hi Catie," said Dr. LaQuaglia as he came to see her that Saturday morning. "How are you doing?"

"I'm fine and I really want to go to school on Tuesday."

He laughed and when he looked at me he knew that this was important for many reasons. Catie needed to feel like a regular kid. She needed to have some normalcy in her life. She needed to have some control. And with that one look, I knew that he was going to do everything he could to get her out of the hospital on Monday.

When he came to see her on Sunday, he said that she could have the chest tube removed. Usually one of his residents did that. On that day, Dr. L. did it himself. When the residents came in later that day to check on Catie they were shocked. "I can't remember the last time he removed a chest tube." What can I say? He and Catie had a very special relationship.

The nurses showed me how to help to prevent a pneumothorax from developing. This was fluid in the lungs that could create severe problems. So I would place a pillow on Catie's back and gently pound on her, making sure that this wasn't happening. We were doing everything we could to make sure we got sprung from the hospital the next day.

On Monday when Dr. L. came in, he checked Catie over to decide if she would be able to make the trip home. When he told her she could go, we both started cheering. Our bags were already packed. I grabbed the medicines we would need to bring with us. We were in a cab heading to Penn Station before anyone could try to stop us. Once we were on the train, we finally relaxed. Until Catie realized that in third grade she should know the multiplication tables.

As we started working on them, I could see the people around us paying attention. The whole train ride home was a lesson in the times tables. The ones, twos and even the threes were pretty easy for her. It was those darn nines that were getting her. I tried to remember all of the little tricks I used but we were still running into problems. Soon we heard "count off your fingers – like 9 x 9 would start on the pinky finger of your right hand. So the pinky finger is number one and then you would count to nine which would end on the ring finger of your left." Bend that finger down and keep it there. You would then have eight on the right side and one on the left equaling 81.

Another passenger had tips on the sevens and another on the eights. Our whole train car spent two and a half hours doing math. I never saw so many happy passengers. They watched Catie concentrating and working so hard. She had told them how she was going to make it to the first day of third grade.

We got off the train in Albany to a chorus of "Good luck, Catie, I know you are going to love third grade." "Catie, you will do great this year, I know it." "Don't forget the tricks you learned about those nine times tables."

I could see them watching Catie, seeing that she was still sore from surgery, but so intent on making it to school. I watched their faces light up with smiles as she practiced her math. I knew that they knew how important this day was. And maybe they were going to go home and watch the school bus come the next day and be grateful for the big things in life, and the little things.

The next morning Catie was at the bus stop with her little brother Robby. She had to carefully hold her backpack because she was still sore from the surgery. But she was so happy to be making it to school. Larry and I stood there proudly, watching her climb on the bus. We waited until the bus was out of sight to cry. We knew how lucky we were to have this first day of third grade.

When I picked her up from school a few hours later, she said, "See, Mom, I did it. I made it to the first day of school!" And all I could think of was if only strength and optimism could cure cancer, maybe, just maybe, we would be seeing many more first days of school.

Chapter 25

Puppy Love

We are a dog family. We like big furry ones. It was okay if they started out small and furry, but they needed to grow to become big ones. And we haven't always been sensible when it came to adding dogs to our family. We knew, however, when Catie was sick, that the presence of a dog could be healing. There is nothing like a puppy in the house to make everyone feel better.

Catie had received a stuffed animal husky and sled to go with her American Girl dolls. She took one look at that dog and was hooked. She kept asking if we could get a real husky. At this time, we already had two golden retrievers. Our first dog, Brandy, had puppies when Catie was three and we ended up keeping one. So we already had two big dogs. More importantly, we were still trying to find more treatment options for Catie. At this point, her prognosis was not good and we didn't know where we would be traveling next for treatment. I did not want another dog. We had enough.

"Mom, Dad and I are going out for a while. We'll be back later."

"Okay, honey. Where are you going?"

"Oh, just out. We won't be too long."

When they got back home they immediately went to the computer. Watching them huddled over the screen, I knew something was up. "What's going on, guys?"

"Oh, nothing" they said in unison. But they both looked guilty. I knew something was up.

The following weekend, Johnny, Robby and I were invited to join them on their road trip. As we headed through Schenectady, I asked, "Where are we going?'

"You'll see."

As we pulled up in front of a nondescript house, I could hear dogs barking the minute we got out of the car. All three kids had smiles on their faces. I could sense an ambush. We knocked on the door and a middle-aged man let us into his house. And there, in a pen near the family room, was a litter of the cutest Siberian huskies I had ever seen. With their black, gray and white coats and blue eyes, they were stunning. But I still thought I had a chance of saying no.

When we got home, we all had a talk about a new dog. "You know guys, a dog is a lot of work and we already have two."

"Mom, we will take turns walking her, really." *Yeah, right.*

"Well, you know, huskies are part wolf. I don't think they are good with kids."

"Well, Mom, that is a common misperception. They are not part wolf and they are very good with children," Catie responded as she showed me her research.

"Give me a week to think about it, okay?" I asked Catie.

"Sure, Mom. Take your time. But I think you would love one."

The following weekend, Lynn and Kevin were coming for a visit. Catie had already filled Kevin in on the puppy issue and the two kids had planned to talk us into another dog visit. The minute they arrived, the kids started in. "Can we go just look at the puppies? Really, Mom, just look, I promise."

"Okay, let's go."

So we all piled in the car and headed to Rotterdam. The minute we walked in the door, the kids went crazy with excitement. They were laughing and petting the puppies and picking them up and dropping them (accidentally). One little female puppy was particularly cute. She and Catie seemed to bond immediately. I looked at Catie and knew I was in trouble. I could see Lynn looking at Kevin, seeing his happiness and excitement. Even she was wavering and she absolutely did not want a dog.

I looked over at Catie's smiling face. Knowing what we were facing, that a cure for her was probably out of the question, I looked at Larry and made the universal hand signal that says, "Pay the man." Larry whipped out the checkbook and we got us a puppy. Maybe not the wisest decision, considering that we already had two big dogs and were looking to find a treatment that might prolong Catie's life. But it was a great decision because now Catie and the boys had a furry, howling, noisy distraction and we all fell in love with her.

Then the problem arose – what do we name her? Catie, a huge Harry Potter fan, thought maybe Hermione, but we weren't too sure about that. She didn't want to name her Harry, so she came up with Potter Gryffindor. At this time, Catie and J.K. Rowling were emailing each other frequently. Catie asked Jo what she thought. Jo loved the name, but when Catie told her that Potter howled all night, Jo asked "Are you sure she's not part wolf?"

Remy, our younger golden retriever decided that he was Potter's babysitter. Remy would lie on the back deck with Potter nestled on his front paws. As Potter continued to grow, we all fell in love with her. Three dogs. What were we thinking!

Now Catie knew that in the American Girl book she read, the husky was a working dog, a sled dog. She wanted to make sure that Potter was a true husky, one that could pull a sled. We looked around to see what we had for Potter to pull. We saw the Kettle Car – a low-to-the-ground vehicle that had pedals to make it move. It looked perfect. So we hooked up Potter to the go-kart, Catie climbed in and off she went. We were all howling with delight as the Southwood Drive Iditarod was born.

The kids were in love with Potter. Even I fell in love with her. It was hard not to. When I looked at Catie's beaming face, there was no doubt in my mind that we did the right thing. So while you can't always get want you want, sometimes you get what you need. And it looks like we needed a dog. Puppy love. It's a beautiful thing.

Chapter 26

Hey Dude

When Catie was diagnosed with cancer, we made a commitment as a family to enjoy whatever came our way. We wanted to make the best of each day. With Catie that was an easy task.

She was a great teacher.

Catie's relapse off of the N7 protocol meant that a cure was almost impossible. At that point, Larry and I decided that we would try anything that wouldn't harm her. We weren't going to put her through high-dose chemotherapy again. We wanted her to come home, enjoy school, see her friends. That didn't mean we had given up hope.

When I think of what we gave her – thalidomide, arsenic and any chemo that was not too toxic – it astounds me. Each treatment started off with hope. With every unfavorable post-treatment scan, we would look around for something else. Our doctors were wonderful in always finding something to try. But we finally realized that there was really nothing left, so we went home and asked for Hospice services.

Catie was going to school when she could. She loved running around with the dogs and seeing her friends. One day I looked out the window and there she was – tearing around in the ravine with the dogs chasing her. I thought, *This is crazy.* I called Dr. Kramer in New York.

"Hi Kim, it's Gina. How are you doing?"

"I'm doing fine. How's our girl?"

"Well, you are not going to believe this. She is running around, playing with the dogs, going to school. I don't know what's happening, but I think maybe we should start looking at options again."

"Fantastic – when can you get down here?"

So two days later we headed back to Sloan-Kettering where the doctors had done even more research. They couldn't believe how good she looked and said, "Let's do scans and see where we are."

"Hi Gina and Catie. The scans don't look any worse from a few months ago and guess what? Duke University has an MIBG treatment. We think it might be right for you. What do you think? asked Kim.

We enthusiastically said, "Let's do it," and the doctors got to work – calling the doctors at Duke, getting our records ready to be sent. When I had a chance, I spoke with Dr. Kramer.

"Kim, what does this mean?"

"Well, Gina, this is not a cure. At best it will be palliative, but we may be able to buy us some time. It's not going to hurt her and watching her run around and look so good makes me think this is the right decision."

So we signed Catie off of Hospice and made our plans. We bought matching pajamas. I gathered craft supplies. We would probably be down there for three weeks or so. We needed to be ready.

"Hey Kim, before we head to do Duke, do you think it's okay if we take a short vacation while you guys work out all of the details. We want to take the kids to a Dude Ranch."

"Absolutely, Gina. Go and have fun. We will have things all ready by the time you get back."

The Pinegrove Dude Ranch is a great family resort. They had boating, horseback riding, an indoor pool and all kinds of activities.

The first thing Catie wanted to do was go horseback riding. We all saddled up and went for a ride, which was really more like a walk. Larry and I were toward the front, the kids were behind us. There was a leader and someone following at the end, so we were well-covered. Except for our daredevil daughter. As we looked back to check on them, Catie had her horse off the trail and was heading up a mountain. She was grinning and loving it.

"Catie, get down here. What are you doing?"

"Aw, Mom, this is fun. Can't I go up the mountain? I'm not afraid. My horse likes me."

"Sorry kiddo, not going to happen. Get over here."

Back at the ranch, we took a boat ride and a tractor-pulled wagon ride. We played bingo and swam. They even had a race in the indoor pool and Robby and Catie won. They were so proud.

When people saw our kids and saw our thin, bald, but very happy daughter, we got a lot of sympathetic looks and kind words. "But she is going to be okay, right?" they would ask, hopefully.

And we would shake our heads and say, "No." They looked on in disbelief that this little girl, who was tearing around, happy as anything, was not going to survive this disease.

"But how can that be? Look at her. She looks so happy and energetic."

"Yes. She is happy and energetic and for right now, that is more than enough."

As we headed home after our four-day vacation, we were so

grateful to have had this time, to create the memories. For four days we were just a regular family. What a gift.

A few days later, Catie woke up with a headache. I said "Honey, I am going to make an appointment with the pediatrician. It's probably just a sinus infection."

If only …

Chapter 27

Heartbreak

It was late April of 2000. Catie and I were almost ready to go to Duke for her experimental treatment. We had already packed our matching pajamas and were gathering our craft supplies. Catie was excited to be going on another adventure. But she had a headache. I called our pediatrician's office and asked if I could bring her in.

"Hi Dr. Gaston. Thanks for seeing us so quickly. Catie has been doing pretty well. We are getting ready to head to Duke for the MIBG treatment. But she's got a headache and I thought we should get it checked out before we head to North Carolina. I think it's probably a sinus infection."

Our pediatrician ushered us into one of the exam rooms. The whole office knew what was going on with Catie and had been so supportive.

"So, Catie, how is it going?"

"Great, except for this headache. We're getting packed to go to Duke."

"Okay, let's take a look."

A few minutes later, the doctor turned to me and said, "I think maybe you should go to Albany Med and have a CT of her head. We want to find out what's going on, what's causing this headache."

"Okay. We'll head down right now."

Feeling calm, which was unlike me, I went to Wendy's drive-through and grabbed a burger. I felt guilty stopping but figured we could be at the hospital for a long time and I was really hungry. Catie wasn't too hungry. She got something to drink.

We headed to Albany Med where the doctors were waiting for us. They took Catie in to be scanned. I gave a quick call to Larry to tell him that she was having a head CT. I made it clear to the hospital staff that this was not an oncology issue, that Catie's doctors were at Sloan-Kettering. I was still calm and nonchalant – why, I don't know. A short while later, the radiologist came out to talk to me.

"Mrs. Hoch, I'm so sorry to tell you this. The cancer is in Catie's brain."

As every hope and dream shattered, I felt like I couldn't breathe. I turned around so Catie wouldn't see me cry, letting the hallway wall hold me up. I called Larry. "It's in her brain."

"I'm on my way."

I called my parents and sister in Florida. Trying to keep my voice steady, I said, "Dad, the cancer is in Catie's brain. You guys should get on the next plane to Albany."

Larry showed up within minutes and we went in to the room where the nurse had taken Catie. "Hey, honey, how are you feeling?"

"I'm okay, Dad, but I still have a headache."

"Okay sweetie, Mom is going to see if we can get you some medicine."

I turned out of the room and went to the desk. "I want pain medication for her and I want it now. I don't want one med student in that room. Not one. Her oncologists are at Sloan-Kettering. No one has permission to see her except for the doctor here."

I called Sloan-Kettering. Dr. Cheung got on the phone.

"What's happening Gina?"

As I tried not to cry I said, "The cancer is in her brain. What are we talking about?"

After a brief pause, "Two weeks. I am so sorry. We can medivac her down here and try to make her comfortable."

"Dr. Cheung, I think we need to bring her home. I don't want her to die in New York City away from her family and friends."

"Gina, I fully support your decision. We'll be in touch. Please let me know what we can do for her."

One of the hospital social workers came by to see if we needed anything. I almost wanted to laugh – need anything? Yeah. How about a miracle? How about letting my daughter grow up? How about a cure for cancer? Can you give me that? Feeling the urge to hurt anyone in my path, I just said, "We don't need anything."

When Catie had received Hospice care before, we became close to her social worker. Lynne had a soothing effect on all of us and she and Catie developed a very special relationship. Her calming presence had helped us through many tough situations. She had given me her home number. I called home and asked our babysitter to look in my personal phone book for Lynne's number. I got her answering machine. Fighting back tears, I said, "Lynne, it's in Catie's brain. We have two weeks. Can you get Hospice back to the house?" She later told me she had never received a message like that and when her husband heard it, her work took on a new meaning for him.

When we got home I knew we had to let people know what was happening. I had started a caringbridge site for Catie. It is a free website service for people who are sick and a way to communicate with friends and family without having to make a hundred phone calls. I knew I had to post the news. Although we had known we would be traveling down this road, the reality was breaking our hearts. I couldn't believe I was going to lose my daughter.

April 29, 2000

Hello everyone - We received some devastating news on Thursday. Catie's disease has metastasized to her brain. We are no longer going to Duke. We are staying home and trying to make her comfortable. It probably won't be long now. Please pray for a speedy and painless journey. Our hearts are breaking. Pray that we have the strength to deal with this.

The next day, Dr. Kramer called. "Gina, bring Catie down here. We can get her to the prom." I could hear the catch in her voice.

"Kim, she is already losing her memory. We want her home, we want her with her family, her friends."

"I understand, but if you change your mind at any time and want her to come down, we are here for her."

April 30, 2000

We are all home now, making the most of each day. We can't believe this is happening. Please pray for a speedy and painless journey for Catie. She probably won't be with us much longer. And pray that Larry and I have the strength to give her up. We are heartbroken.

We were staying home. Home where Catie could be with family and friends, where she could play and chat and visit. I emailed Jo Rowling to let her know that we were near the end. And I couldn't believe when she asked if it would be okay for her to call the house. She wanted to read to Catie from the yet unfinished Book 4 of the Harry Potter series. We set up a time and watched in joy and amazement as Catie lay on the couch while J.K. Rowling read to her. The next time she called, Jo asked "So, did you put us on speakerphone?"

I laughed and said "Actually we didn't. We just all sat around in the living room watching Catie talk to you. And boy, was she happy."

We tried to keep things normal. We let Catie set the pace. When she felt well enough to get out of bed, she got out of bed. One day, she was feeling really well. We had only been home a few days and the Hospice nurse was coming. She was going to have to unhook Catie from her meds for an hour. When the nurse arrived, we looked at Catie and Catie looked at us and we said, "We're out of here."

Catie had been wanting to get some new clothes for her American Girl dolls. While the nurse looked at us with her mouth agape, we told her, "We'll be back in an hour." We carried Catie to the car and sped to Michael's craft store. We spent most of the hour buying doll clothes.

That night, Robby asked, "Mom, is Catie going to die?"

"Yes honey, she is. We are not going to talk about in front of Catie because we don't want to make her sad. But you can go in the room any time you want to talk to her and play with her. She loves you very much."

As I sank down into a chair in the bedroom on the first floor, with my head in my hands, I thought, *What kind of world is this that I have to tell my son that his sister is dying?* And then I thought of Catie's happy face as she picked out new clothes for her dolls on our little outing. And I thought, *Please let me look at life the way Catie does. Let me enjoy each minute. I have the best teacher in the world. Please let me learn from her.*

Chapter 28

The Best Day Of My Life

Sometimes the best days come at the most unexpected times. Catie was a master at finding those times.

After learning the news that the cancer had spread to her brain, we set up Catie in the downstairs bedroom. This way, she didn't have to keep going up and down the stairs to go to bed and I was closer to her medicine that needed to be refrigerated. When friends or family visited, we were right there on the first floor.

Catie was on a lot of pain and anxiety medication. Some were oral medications, but most were intravenous. I had to insert a needle with a syringe into the vial and pull the plunger to get the medicine into it. I drew up as many vials as I could in advance. I lined up the ones that had to be kept cold on the door of the fridge. The others I drew up, labeled, put into plastic bags and thumbtacked them to the wall in the bedroom. I needed to get to them as quickly as possible. Hospice was back in.

Our goal was to make her as comfortable and happy as possible for the time we had left. Each day we awoke not knowing if it would be our last with her. Some days, she wasn't feeling well and spent most of the day in bed. But other days, she awoke with a smile and enough energy to have some fun. Catie was our teacher, showing us what it really meant to make the most of each day.

I tried to match her enthusiasm and energy, but I was having a tough time. One night I took a short break from being by Catie's side so that I could spend a few minutes with Robby and Johnny. I knew that they were receiving love and attention from all of the family around us, but I needed to be there for them too. Robby and Johnny were in the bathtub and I was reading a book to them. I could hear Catie's little voice, "Mommy, I need you." I said, "I'll be right down, honey. Just give me a few minutes." I tried to read for another minute, but she kept calling to me. As I sat on the edge of the tub, I put my head in my hands and thought, *I don't know if I can do this.*

Robby looked up at me and said, "It's okay Mom. We will read it another day."

We settled into our new routine. I don't think I ever left the first floor of our house after that. Catie seemed to be able to face each day with joy. The Sunday after we learned the news, she woke up with a smile, excited to face the day.

"Morning, Mom, what are we going to do today?"

"Well honey, Kevin and Lynn are coming over. Kevin wants to wear his tux. He asked if you could put on your blue prom dress. Then tonight we are going to go to the Japanese steakhouse with them. How does that sound?"

"Great. I can't wait to see Kevin. He said he is going to bring his new camera. He wants to have a photo shoot."

"Sounds perfect, Catie. It should be lots of fun."

A few minutes later Catie turned to me and asked, "What are we going to do today?"

My heart sank and my eyes filled with tears as I repeated what

I had just told her. I knew the cancer was taking over her brain, that she was losing her memory.

A short while later, Lynn and Kevin showed up. He had a garment bag with his tuxedo in it and a camera slung over his shoulder. Lynn and I hugged fiercely. No words were needed.

"Hi Catie. I'm so happy to see you. I thought maybe we could take some pictures and then put on our prom clothes for some other pictures." Kevin loved photography. Catie loved to be with him. They made such a cute couple.

"Sounds great to me. Let's start in my room." And off they went. We laughed at the two of them.

Lynn knew that we were just trying to hold it together. There isn't much to say when your child's best friend is dying. We both knew that our time to grieve would come. Right now it was Catie and Kevin's day. We were going to do everything possible to make it perfect.

Catie put on her prom dress. Kevin got into his tux. They looked adorable. A few months before, Catie wanted to pick out her prom dress for this year. With hope in my heart, we pored over catalogs and flipped through pages. Finally she found just the one she wanted. It was a pale blue satin dress with a taffeta skirt. She wanted to make sure that when she spun around, the dress would twirl. As I ordered that dress, I prayed that she would make it to the prom.

Just like preparing for a high school prom, we took photos of the kids in the family room and out in the backyard. Someone grabbed a bunch of flowers and made a bouquet for Catie. Robby and Johnny were running around laughing. My parents were making sure everyone was comfortable. My friend Fran showed up with a fruit platter. Before we knew it, we were having a party.

The kids of course had to play with Potter. Kevin had visited Potter with us when we went to the breeder. He and Catie determined that when they got older, they would raise huskies. Catie decided that she had to show Kevin that Potter was really a sled dog. So we hooked Potter up to the kettle car and she took off. With a smile as big as the sky, she went flying down the street with Kevin chasing them. Then it was his turn and we watched in amazement as Catie chased him. It was another Southwood Drive Iditarod.

As evening approached the kids got changed and we headed to our favorite local Japanese restaurant. Catie and Kevin ordered frothy sweet drinks. The chef, who had gotten to know Catie, outdid himself with the chopping and flinging food. He kept tossing food to Larry who was determined to catch it . Even if it meant falling off of his chair. Which he did. With a smile. And the kids laughed hysterically.

That night as Catie and I lay in bed chatting, she turned to me and said, "Mom, I think I have a crush on Kevin."

"Cate, to me a crush is when you see a cute boy across the room and think you might want to talk to him. I think what you have with Kevin is love. You know each other really well, you take care of each other and what you have is so special. I don't think it's a crush. I think it's love."

"Really?"

"Yup, really."

I sent a silent thank you to Kevin, for coming into Catie's life, for being such a good friend and for giving her a taste of what it is like to love someone.

She turned to me with a big grin and said, "Mom, this was the best day of my life."

I looked at her and thought, *Oh dear God, please give me the strength to be able to say goodbye to my beautiful daughter. Please help me be more like Catie.*

Chapter 29

Ladybugs And Good-Bye

Once we learned that the cancer had gone to Catie's brain, our world had shrunk down to the guest bedroom on the first floor, the bathroom and the kitchen. Most days, Catie lay in bed. We watched television or we read to her. Every time she felt anxious or was in pain, the medicine was right there. I made sure it would only take me a few seconds to get the drugs into her system.

I read a couple of books to her about children and death, but she didn't seem very interested in them. Catie wanted to watch the Rugrats Mother's Day video. The one where Chuckie learns from his dad that his mom had left him a letter before she died. And in that letter his mom told Chuckie that she would always be with him. Even when he couldn't see her, she would be with him. This was the video that Catie wanted to watch over and over. I know that she was sending me a message.

At one point I turned to her and asked "Catie, when one of us is gone, how will the one still living know that the other one is still around?"

Without a second's hesitation, she turned to me and said "Mom, every time you see a ladybug, you will know that I am with you." I know that she knew that she was dying. And that she wanted to protect me. And it was breaking my heart.

Catie was slowly sleeping more and more. She wasn't eating much and she wasn't too agitated. One morning, very early, I snuck out of the bedroom and went to the kitchen to have a cup of tea. It felt like I was coming out of a cave. As I sat there for a few minutes I heard a little voice calling "Mommy, Mommy."

I raced to open the kitchen door and found Catie on the floor in the hallway. She had tried to go to the bathroom herself and had fallen and broken her front teeth. The only reason she wasn't in a lot of pain was because of the amount of fentanyl, a very strong narcotic, in her system. I carried her back to bed. Larry looked at our beautiful daughter with her broken teeth and walked out the back door. He sat on the steps to the deck, sobbing. "We are losing our little girl piece by piece."

I called our dentist to let him know, not really sure if he could or would do anything. Later that day he came to the house and made a mold of her teeth. The day after, he came back with new teeth for her. It meant so much to us to have her put back together, even a little bit.

Catie then started lapsing into a coma-like state. She would sleep for hours. She wasn't restless or in pain, but she wasn't responding to us either. I would lay next to her, with my hand on her head. I was reading a book and didn't absorb one word of it. One morning she woke up and said with a weak smile "I didn't die yet" and then went back to sleep. I wasn't sure how much more we could take.

Later that same day, Catie woke up with a smile. "Mom, can you invite all my friends over today? I really want to see them."

"Of course honey" I said as Larry and I looked at each other, wondering what was going on. After several frantic calls to her friends and cousin, the girls all arrived, waiting to see Catie. They were all sitting around in the kitchen when Catie came out of the bedroom. They started chattering away and then Catie said "I want to give you each one of my American Girl dolls."

Catie loved her American Girl dolls. We had read all the books and every time a new accessory was added to her collection, we spent hours oohing and aahing over them. One of our favorite things was to go on e-bay and shop for new clothes for the dolls. We all looked on in disbelief as Catie gave each girl one of her beloved dolls. A few minutes later she said "I think I'm getting tired so I am going to go back to bed. Bye guys."

After that, Catie spent most of her time sleeping. I was in the bed with her and Larry slept on the floor. We would tell her how much we loved her and how it was okay to go. Of course it would never be okay, but we wanted her to feel peaceful. At one point she looked at us and with a beatific smile on her face said "It's so beautiful." We like to think she got a glimpse of heaven.

We had spent almost no time with Robby and Johnny for the last several days. We sent Robby off to school, he was in first grade, but Johnny was just four and he needed a break. My parents and sisters were at the house and took care of everything that we couldn't. They were watching the boys and giving them love and attention, but Larry wanted to spend a little time with Johnny while Robby was at school.

"Honey, I am going to take Johnny and a friend to McDonald's for a little while. I really feel like he needs some attention" said Larry

"Yeah, go ahead. We are okay here. Things are status quo. Bring him out – it's a great idea."

About a half hour after he left, I noticed a change in Catie's breathing. Her breaths were coming slower and were getting raspy. I placed my hand on her head and watched her breathe. And as I told her that I loved her, she took her last breath. I lay next to her and couldn't believe that she was gone. That I wasn't going to be able to watch my girl grow up, fight with me, go to college, get married, have children.

I thought *How am I going to live without her?* And then I remembered a conversation Catie had with one of her friends.

The kids were sitting in the back of the car and her friend asked "Catie, if there was one thing you could change about your life, what would it be?"

"I wouldn't change a thing" she said. "Not even having cancer, because of the places I got to go, the things I learned and the friends I made. Nope, I wouldn't change a thing."

As I lay in bed next to my daughter I thought *How did I get so lucky? I got to be Catie's mom.*

Chapter 30

A Life Well-Lived

Larry and I knew that Catie's services would have to reflect her personality. There were to be no sad readings or black clothing. We wanted everyone to remember the joyful child who changed our world. At the wake, where hundreds of people came to pay their respects, the boom box was playing the Backstreet Boys. Her third grade class came to us, bearing yellow roses. As I looked at their little faces, I just knew in my heart that Catie made a lasting impact on them.

On the morning of her funeral, I sat on the bed, crying. I looked at Larry and said "I can't do this."

He said, "Yes you can. Catie would want you to."

I put on my floral print dress that I know Catie would have loved and we headed to church. The priest knew that we wanted joy and color and light on that day. No "walking through the valley of the shadow of death." This was a celebration of a life well-lived. A life far too short, but an amazing life in the time she had with us.

My sister and her friend had painted Catie's casket with ladybugs, a labor of love if there ever was one. As my family said goodbye to our daughter, I watched the sadness on their faces. But as memories were shared, I saw the smiles and laughter. I knew that would have made Catie happy.

I also knew the years ahead were going to be difficult – the first time we asked for a table for four instead of five, the first Christmas without her, her birthday, the anniversary of her death. But sprinkled throughout the pain was a sense of joy. Because Catie could look at any situation and find the good in it, she left us with that lesson.

Anyone who knew Catie knew what a bright, bubbly, happy, optimistic child she was. How she could turn hearing aids and surgeries and radioactive isolation into an adventure was inspiring. Her smile rarely left her face. Even as she was living out her last few days, she was thinking of others. She wanted to help other kids have fun.

I know that she was worried about me, that she wanted to protect me. When she told me that every time I saw a ladybug I would know she was with me, she gave me an everlasting gift. I cannot see a ladybug without smiling. People who never met her but who know the story tell me about their ladybug sightings and how good that made them feel.

This little girl, in nine short years, changed our lives. And she changed them for the better. I try to be grateful for what I have. I try to see the good in difficult situations. I try to make sure that kids with cancer have the resources to have some fun. Every day I am thankful for Catie. She was the best teacher I could ever have.

Epilogue

The Magic Continues

Throughout the years, Catie has continued to make her presence known. Often when we needed it most. Sometimes it brought tears to our eyes, but many times it brought smiles. And the sight of a ladybug always brings comfort.

When Larry and I established the Catie Hoch Foundation in 2000, Catie was very much a part of the foundation and was excited about it. And looking back I see that she knew she was going to die, and that she wanted to have a say in things.

"Mom, if things get written about me, I want them to say Catie. And I want the name of the foundation to be the Catie Hoch Foundation, not Catherine Hoch."

"Okay, Catie. Whatever you want." Larry and I looked at each other and we knew what she was talking about. She wanted her headstone to say Catie, not Catherine. We had tears in our eyes, unable to believe how much strength she had. She was facing her death with such courage.

The foundation was to be her legacy. We knew we wanted to keep her memory alive.

We knew that we wanted to help children while they were in treatment. We knew that the foundation was going to be a good thing when so many donations were made in Catie's memory.

Life without Catie was heartbreaking and challenging. We were devastated, but we were trying to do what was right for the boys. And ladybug sightings brought us comfort. A few weeks after Catie died, we took the kids bowling. Robby was seven and Johnny four. It was early Sunday morning and the bowling alley had been cleaned the night before. As we were getting ready to bowl, I looked down and saw something.

"Guys, look at this." I said.

On the newly cleaned carpet was a sticker. One sticker, one ladybug sticker. I smiled and sent Catie a silent hello.

Larry and I weren't sure what kind of fundraising would be best for the Catie Hoch Foundation. We invited friends and family to a first meeting. One of our friends asked "What would you guys think of doing a 5K right here in the neighborhood?"

"What a great idea," I said. "Does anyone know anything about hosting a 5K?"

The response was a whole bunch of no's, but that didn't stop them. By the next meeting we had a plan.

Our first Catiebug for a Cure was held in in our development in Clifton Park five months after Catie died. We raised over $30,000 and more than 200 people came out to support us. It was a bittersweet day. I was filled with gratitude, watching so many people run in her memory, but I was missing her so much. And then I looked down at my sweatshirt. And what was sitting there on a cold, blustery October day? Of course, a ladybug.

The following December, Kevin was dying. He and Catie were truly soulmates. I would often head over to Pittsfield. Lynn had told me that many times Kevin had been having very vivid dreams about Catie. Kevin would recount them to his mom during the night and in the morning.

"Hey Kev. How are you doing, honey?"

"Hi Gina. I'm okay. Did my Mom tell you that I keep seeing Catie in my dreams?"

"She did tell me. So what did Catie have to say? How is she? How does she look?" I asked.

"Well, she's doing fine. She misses you, but she's good. She looks great too. Pretty much the same, but she has her hair and she's got wings!"

"What else did she have to say?"

"Well, she wanted to know if I was ready to go and I told her not yet. So she told me there are a few ways to get to heaven. You can take an elevator. Mary can bring you up. Or you can take an escalator. She also gave me a tour. She told me that first time I go into heaven, I have to go through the big gates. Then she showed me a side door. Once you are in, you can go in and out of that door without going through the big ones."

I had to smile. *Escalators and side doors.* That sure sounded like Catie.

Kevin died in December of 2001. Larry and I went to his memorial service in the huge gymnasium of the school he'd attended. We listened to so many people who loved him.

I talked about Kevin and Catie and their antics. Throughout the service we kept seeing something small flying around the gym. It was, of course, a ladybug. In a cold, drafty gym. In the middle of December.

A few months later, I shared with Lynn one of my fears.

"Every time we hold a fundraiser, I feel like I'm losing a little bit of Catie. I'm not sure this is the right thing for me to be doing."

"Gina, I think Catie would be proud of what you are doing."

A few minutes later, after we hung up, my doorbell rang. A messenger was delivering a letter from Scotland. *Scotland?* I opened the letter and I cried. It said that the Catie Hoch Foundation was receiving a $100,000 donation from J.K. Rowling. I called Lynn and told her what happened.

"Are you really thinking you're not doing the right thing?"

she said. "I'd say this is a big sign that Catie is happy with what you're doing."

In January of 2009, cancer struck again when Larry was diagnosed with a malignant brain tumor.

"How could your family be hit twice?" people asked us.

We had no answer for that. We just knew that we were going to fight it as hard as we could. With Catie's wisdom to guide us, Larry went through surgery, many many rounds of radiation and a stem cell transplant. He was on chemo for three and a half years. When we faltered, when fear took over, we would think about Catie and what she endured.

Often the sight of a ladybug brought us such comfort and hope. Once, while waiting for an MRI at Albany Medical Center, we spotted a book cart. It was the cart that the Catie Hoch Foundation had donated to the pediatric department. And there it was, painted all over with ladybugs. Larry had good results with that MRI.

Although Larry fought every day, with everything he had, his cancer continued to spread.

He was in the hospital for a week in the Spring of 2012. He came home on Hospice. Larry died in July. Once again I said goodbye to someone I loved. Someone who should have had many more years on this earth.

The day after his death, my nieces and nephew came to our house to see me. We shared stories about Larry for hours – his legendary appetite, his sense of humor, his kindness. Around 11 p.m. as they were leaving, my niece stopped short at the door and did a double-take. "Aunt Gina, you have got to see this!"

"Amy, what's up?"

There on my screen door were two ladybugs, just hanging out. We smiled through our tears, knowing that Catie was with her Dad and that they both were saying "hi."

This past December a horrific accident on the Northway killed two kids and seriously injured two others. I knew the uncle of the boy kids killed in the crash. He sent a note, telling me that one day he was looking at his nephew's prayer card and saying a rosary with an online group.

When he looked down, he saw a ladybug sitting on that prayer card and that ladybug stayed there until he finished the rosary. He said the sight of that ladybug brought him such comfort, that he felt Catie was watching out for his nephew. This man never met Catie, but he knew her story.

My boys and I were facing new challenges, learning to reconfigure our lives.

With Robby in college and Johnny a high school senior, we knew that at some point changes would need to be made. The house where the boys grew up would be much too big for me alone and the maintenance would be overwhelming. We had a small camp on a nearby lake. I knew I wasn't going to be able to go to the camp again. There were too many beautiful memories of us with our friends, relaxing on the deck, drinking beer and eating good food. Larry loved his time at the camp. I had no desire to be there without him.

The boys thought I should sell both the house and the camp. They thought a townhouse near the lake would be perfect for us. I didn't think I was ready for that much change so soon.

In November of 2012, a friend invited me to "just look" at townhouses. I had absolutely no intention of buying. Until I walked into the second townhouse I saw. I loved it. I brought the boys to see it and they fell in love with it too. But what sealed the deal was what we saw as we were about to leave. There above the front door were five ladybugs. Yes, five ladybugs for the five of us – Larry, Catie, Robby, Johnny and me. I truly believe that Catie and Larry led us to our new home.

On Catie's headstone its says, "Some people come into our lives and quickly go. Others stay for a while and leave footprints on our hearts and we are never, ever the same."

Catie changed our world forever.

Catie's Recipe
For Getting Better

You will get better
You need a good hospital
You need 7 cups of chemo
You need 10 spoons of patience
You need 5 eggs of strength
1 spoon of Game Boy color
A pinch of fruit rollup
10 cups of Benadryl
5 cups of Antibodies
A spoon of oreos
10 cups of popcorn
100 bowls of Little Shop of Plaster
25 cups of the Brady Bunch
2 scoops of butter pecan ice cream
100 cups of friends because it makes it more fun
100 bowls of FAO Schwarz!

Praise for *I Wouldn't Change a Thing*

Kim Kramer, MD, Co-Director of Pediatric Neuro-Oncology at Memorial Sloan-Kettering writes:

> Thousands of children are diagnosed with cancer each year, and parents frequently document their journey, especially in today's era of blogs and social media. It is quite possible that Gina Peca, in recalling her daughter Catie's battle with a rare illness called neuroblastoma, has the most unique and eloquent approach to expressing the many stages of dealing with a child's life threatening illness: shock, denial, anger, frustration, depression, and ultimate acceptance. With poignant recollections of all those involved in Catie's journey, she gives the reader incredible insight as to how childhood cancer affects the patient, parents, siblings, extended family, and the many medical and social professionals involved. Catie's physical journey ended with her death in 2000 but her story, told through the eyes of her loving mother, is one that is very much alive with hope.

Joan O'Hanlon Curry, Nurse Practitioner at Sloan-Kettering during Catie's treatment:

> I was honored to be part of the team who took care of Catie and her family. Catie was an incredibly smart, funny and insightful kid. This disease impacts the whole family, not just the patient and Gina and Larry handled this with immense grace and courage. Every patient is special but Catie had that extra something that drew people in and made an everlasting impression. This book gives you an idea of what the cancer journey is like and what we do as caregivers to make a difference.

Tom Schreck, author of the ***Duffy Dombrowski Mysteries***. *The Vegas Knockout* was an Amazon #1 Best Selling Hard-Boiled Mystery.

> Gina Peca's, I Wouldn't Change A Thing, her memoir of her cherished life with her cancer- stricken daughter, is all at once uplifting, heartbreaking and, most of all, inspiring. Catie's poignant story is far more than a recounting of a mother's loss and instead offers all of us a lesson in living a joyful life through the sparkly eyes of a child who knew, felt and shared how to live every moment to its fullest.